How to Use thi...

1 Read the question at the top of the page

2 Slide the peg to the letter of the answer

3 Finish all the questions on that page

then flip it over

and see how many you got right!

Repeat on the next page, and the next, and the next, and so on..... **go!**

D

1. Why do fireflies blink their lights?

TO ATTRACT A MATE

Everyone needs a little attention. They're trying to look as flashy as possible.

HEY! LOOK OVER HERE!

B

2. Which of these kills more people?

MOSQUITOES

Mosquitoes can carry malaria, and that disease kills one to two million people every year.

C

3. Which of these isn't really an insect?

A SPIDER

Technically, you need six legs to be an insect. A spider's got eight legs. If you've got eight legs, you're an arachnid. Just like scorpions and ticks.

B

4. How long can a healthy worker ant expect to live?

6 MONTHS

Being an ant is no picnic. If you live past half a year, you're a geezer ant. And the worst part? You never get a birthday present.

A

5. Why do moths go crazy over porch lights?

THEY THINK IT'S THE MOON.

Moths find their way by using the moon, and our lights confuse their little brains.

1 Why do fireflies blink their lights?

A to see where they are going

C because they're afraid of the dark

B to attract smaller bugs to eat

D to attract a mate

2 Which of these kills more people?

A bees

C cockroaches

B mosquitoes

D very, very angry ladybugs

3 Which of these isn't really an insect?

A a pear slug

C a spider

B an ox warble fly

D a thrip

4 How long can a healthy worker ant expect to live?

A 4 days

C 1 year

B 6 months

D 7 hours

5 Why do moths go crazy over porch lights?

A They think it's the moon.

C They want to see their food better.

B They're chilly and need the warmth.

D They really like slam dancing.

B

6. Where is the largest bone in your body found?

your thigh

The long bone that goes from your hip to your knee is called the femur. It is also the strongest bone in your body. (I hope so. It has to carry you around all day.)

C

7. Where are the smallest bones?

your ear

There are three little bones in each of your ears. They carry the vibrations from your ear drum into your inner ear, then to your brain. That is, if you're listening.

B

8. What is the most common broken bone?

the clavicle

It's your collarbone. It connects your shoulder to your breastbone. When you fall and reach out with your arms, the weight can break it.

C

9. The two ribs on the bottom of your rib cage are called floating ribs. Why is that?

They're attached to the spine...

in the back but to nothing in the front. The rest of your ribs connect to the spine in back and to something in the front.

A

10. When you're born, you have 275 bones. When you're an adult, you have only 206 bones. What happened to those 69 bones?

Some bones fuse together.

Many of those little bones in your hands and feet fuse together. Also a few of the bones in your head fuse together. That's right, when your were born, your head was flexible.

6 **Where is the largest bone in your body found?**

A your head   **C** your back

B your thigh   **D** your chest

about your skeleton...

7 **Where are the smallest bones?**

A your McNuggets   **C** your ear

B your mouth   **D** your hands

8 **What is the most common broken bone?**

A the cranium   **C** the thumb

B the clavicle   **D** the ankle

9 **The two ribs on the bottom of your rib cage are called floating ribs. Why is that?**

A They help you stay afloat in deep water.

C They're attached to the spine in back but float free in the front.

B They move freely around the body.

D They taste good with root beer.

10 **When you're born, you have 275 bones. When you're an adult, you have only 206 bones. What happened to those 69 bones?**

A Some bones fuse together as you age.

C They turn into muscle.

B They dissolve into the blood stream.

D They're put into a savings account for your retirement.

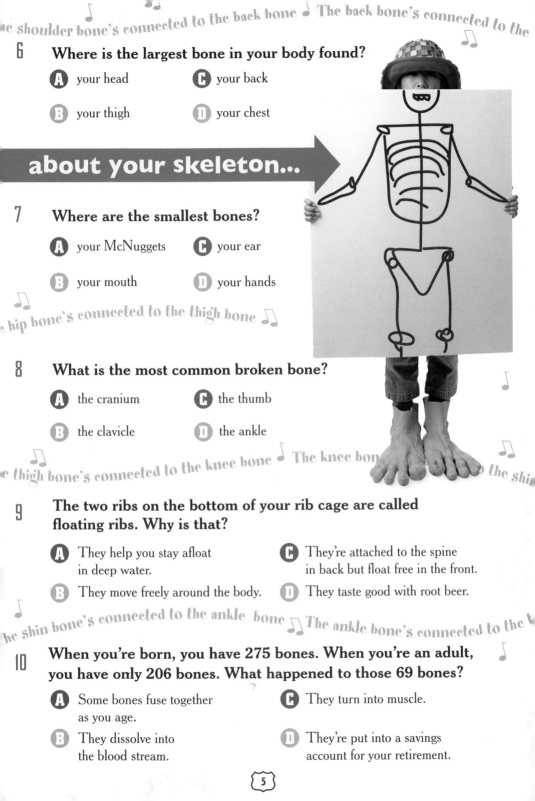

D

11. What do you do with the largest muscle in your body?

sit on it

Your gluteus maximus is the biggest muscle in your body. Be proud. I'm sure you worked hard to make it that way.

D

12. Which of these is NOT a human muscle?

Altoid

Even though they are curiously strong, they're mints and not muscles.

B

13. What is your most valuable muscle?

your heart

Well, it's our favorite at least. And besides, your brain, lungs and ego *aren't* muscles.

D

14. Where is your body's strongest muscle?

your big mouth

It's called the masseter, and it opens and closes your mouth. It's strong to help you chew food.

A

15. The tongue is a special muscle. What makes it different from all the rest?

It's attached only at one end.

That's what allows it to flap around in that big mouth of yours.

11 What do you do with the largest muscle in your body?

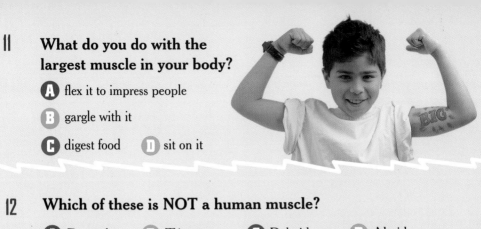

A flex it to impress people

B gargle with it

C digest food **D** sit on it

12 Which of these is NOT a human muscle?

A Pectoral **B** Tricep **C** Deltoid **D** Altoid

Let's talk about your Muscles!

13 What is your most valuable muscle?

A your brain **C** your lungs

B your heart **D** your ego

14 Where is your body's strongest muscle?

A your leg **C** your chest

B your back **D** your big mouth

15 The tongue is a special muscle. What makes it different from all the rest?

A It's attached only at one end. **C** It shrinks when you sleep.

B It moves the fastest. **D** It can say "Mississippi."

B

16. The fastest wild animal in the world is…

the peregrine falcon

The peregrine falcon can dive at speeds over 150 mph.
The cheetah is the fastest on land (70+ mph).

D

17. In English, ducks say "quack quack." In French, they say…

coin coin

In Hebrew, incidentally, ducks say
"gaga gaga."

COIN?
PUT IT
ON MY BILL.

C

18. What kind of huge animal was hunted by early humans several thousand years ago?

mammoths

Unlike dinosaurs, mammoths and humans co-existed for hundreds
of years. The last mammoth died approximately 9,000 years ago, and
well-preserved frozen individuals are still occasionally found in Siberia.

D

19. This is the shape of a camel's spine.

A camel's spine is straight.
The hump is mostly fat,
with no bones.

WHO YOU
CALLIN' FAT?

D

20. Why aren't there any alligator wrestlers in Australia?

There aren't any alligators in Australia.

Alligators live in the Americas and Asia. In Australia, there are
crocodiles. They're similar, but larger and with a narrower snout.

16 The fastest wild animal in the world is...

A the cheetah

C the gazelle

B the peregrine falcon

D the eagle

ANIMAL FACTS

17 In English, ducks say "quack quack."
In French, they say...

HOW INTERESTING.

A bon bon

C chuffa chugga

B oinque oinque

D coin coin

18 What kind of huge animal
was hunted by early humans
several thousand years ago?

A dinosaurs

C mammoths

B condors

D scaly ginormicus

19 This is the shape of a camel's spine.

A   **B**   **C**   **D**

20 Why aren't there any alligator wrestlers in Australia?

A Nobody's brave enough.

C Alligators refuse to wrestle.

B There used to be some,
but they've all been eaten.

D There aren't any alligators
in Australia.

21. *"Happy Birthday" is the most sung song in the world.*

Way!

And 21 people are born every five seconds.
So get ready to hear it again and again
and again...

22. *Some golf balls have honey in their center.*

Way!

Sometimes the sweet spot is really sweet.

23. *Astronauts get 2 inches taller in space.*

Way!

Without gravity you do get taller.
Gravity on Earth at sea level pushes
us down as much as if we had
15 pounds of lead on our heads.

24. *There are 40 cubic feet of dirt in a hole
that is 4 feet by 5 feet and 2 feet deep.*

No way!

There's NO dirt in a hole.
That's what makes it a hole.

25. *Cavemen used to catch and train dinosaurs.*

No way!

It's fun to watch *The Flintstones*, but all the dinosaurs were gone
at least 70 MILLION years before there were cave people.

21 "Happy Birthday" is the most sung song in the world.

A Way! (true) **B** No way! (false)

22 Some golf balls have honey in their center.

A Way! **B** No way!

23 Astronauts get 2 inches taller in space.

A Way! **B** No way!

24 There are 40 cubic feet of dirt in a hole that is 4 feet by 5 feet and 2 feet deep.

A Way! **B** No way!

25 Cavemen used to catch and train dinosaurs.

A Way!

No way!

MONGO WANT T-REX TO FETCH!

C

26. *As the Earth spins, all the stars appear to wheel around the night sky in a giant circle except the...*

North Star

The North Star happens to be located directly above the North Pole and the other stars look like they spin around it.

B

27. *Where do most scientists believe humans originally came from?*

Africa

The oldest human fossils have been found in East Africa, dating from around 150,000 years ago.

C

28. *If you drink H_2O mixed with NaCl, you will...*

feel a little sick

H_2O is water. NaCl is salt. Drinking salt water will make you a little sick and do nothing for your thirst, which is why castaways on life rafts are surrounded by water they can't drink.

C

29. *The blueprint for a human being is contained in a long, twisted helix molecule called...*

DNA

Every single cell in your body contains copies of your unique DNA. Since there is no one else quite like you, there are no copies of it.

B

30. *In the laboratory, if this color liquid mixed with this color liquid you'd get this color liquid...*

GREEN! I'VE DONE IT!

26 As the Earth spins, all the stars appear to wheel around the night sky in a giant circle except the...

A Star of Bethlehem

C North Star

B middle belt star of Orion

D South Star

27 Where do most scientists believe humans originally came from?

A New Jersey

C Asia

B Africa

D Europe

SCIENTIFIC STUFF

28 If you drink H_2O mixed with NaCl, you will...

A gain superpowers

C feel a little sick

B die a horrible death

D feel terrific

29 The blueprint for a human being is contained in a long, twisted helix molecule called...

A IRS

C DNA

B CIA

D IOU

30 In the laboratory, if this color liquid mixed with this color liquid you'd get this color liquid...

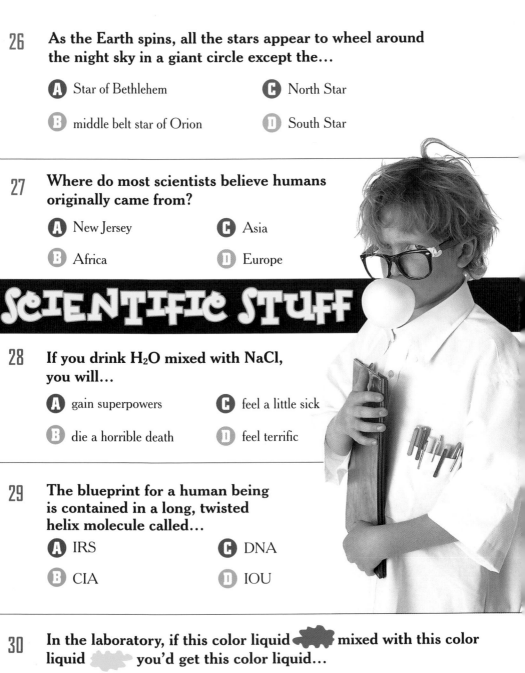

A   **B**   **C**   **D**

B

31. *Elephants are the largest animal on land. The second largest is the rhino. Which of these is number 3?*

the hippo

An adult can weigh over 3 tons. By the way, the blue whale is the largest animal on our planet.

FEED ME.

C

32. *How can you tell an African elephant from an Indian elephant?*

the shape of the ears

An Indian elephant has ears that are smaller and more pointed (shaped like the country of India). An African's are larger and rounder (shaped like the continent of Africa).

D

33. *You just kicked an elephant in the shin. What are your chances of getting away?*

You're toast.

Don't bother to run. Elephants can run faster than 15 mph for a short distance. The world's fastest human can barely reach that speed. Consider yourself flat.

D

34. *What is a rhino's horn made of?*

hair

An elephant's tusks are made of ivory. But the rhino's horn is just densely packed hair.

C

35. *Elephants, hippos and rhinos are all herbivores. If they were all coming to your house for dinner, what should you prepare?*

400 pounds of salad

An herbivore eats only plants. So prepare lots of salad. And prepare to need a new house, too.

GULP!

31 Elephants are the largest animal on land. The second largest is the rhino. Which of these is number 3?

A the giraffe

C the blue whale

B the hippo

D the tyrannosaurus terrier

32 How can you tell an African elephant from an Indian elephant?

A the accent

B the shape of the trunk

C the shape of the ears

D the number of toes

33 You just kicked an elephant in the shin. What are your chances of getting away?

A 100 percent

B pretty good

C about 50-50

D You're toast.

34 What is a rhino's horn made of?

A bone

B skin

C ivory

D hair

Elephants!
and friends

35 Elephants, hippos and rhinos are all *herbivores*. If they were all coming to your house for dinner, what should you prepare?

A three humongous steaks

C 400 pounds of salad

B 400 pounds of fish

D live chickens and vanilla pudding

Yes, Kids, it's time for a
Stupid Vocabulary Quiz!

A

36. mortarboard
Isn't it funny that they make school graduates wear stupid-looking hats? They're called mortarboards.

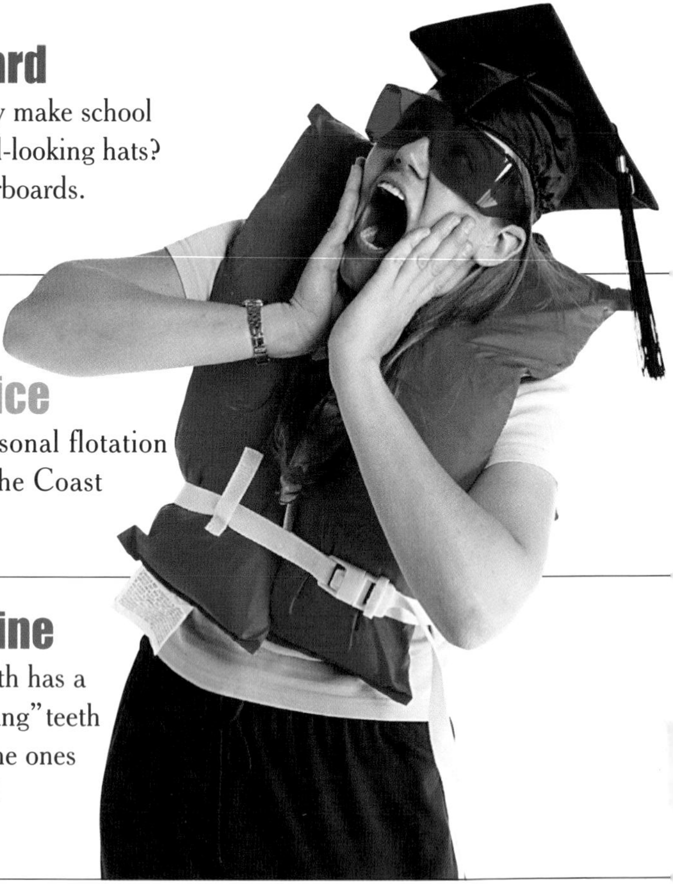

D

37. personal flotation device
The life vest is a personal flotation device or P.F.D. as the Coast Guard calls them.

C

38. lower canine
Every one of your teeth has a name. Your upper "fang" teeth are called canines. The ones below them are called lower canines.

B

39. optical filter
Sunglasses are filters for the eyes, so that makes them optical filters.

yes, kids, it's time for a

Stupid Vocabulary Quiz!

A

B

C

D

36

"mortarboard"

37

"personal flotation device"

38

"lower canine"

39

"optical filter"

D

40. Why do poodles have that funny haircut?

to help them be better swimmers

They got their hair cut short to help them move through the water. But they left the puffs of hair to keep their heart and chests warm.

MY BEST STROKE IS THE DOG PADDLE.

C

41. What dog breed is most popular in the U.S.?

Labrador retrievers

Number 2 is the golden retriever. Number 3 is the German shepherd. And number 4 is the beagle.

C

42. This is a REAL dog breed.

Mexican hairless

It's a medium-sized dog with little to no hair. Which some people think is cute.

IS IT COLD IN HERE OR IS IT JUST ME?

B

43. Your dog's is 1,000 times better than yours.

sense of smell

That's why they're always waiting for you at the door when you come home. They can smell your funk from around the block.

I SMELLED YOU COMIN'!

B

44. These foods are toxic to your dog.

chocolate and onions

So be careful not to let your dog into your cookies or onion rings. In fact, if that's what you're having for lunch, you might feel sick too.

40 **Why do poodles have that funny haircut?**

A to get attention

C It's just how their hair grows.

B They love punk rock.

D to help them be better swimmers

41 **What dog breed is most popular in the U.S.?**

A German shepherds

B golden retrievers

C Labrador retrievers

D beagles

42 **This is a REAL dog breed.**

A Spanish lipless

B Bolivian tailless

C Mexican hairless

D They're all real.

43 **Your dog's is 1,000 times better than yours.**

A eyesight

B sense of smell

C sense of taste

D sense of humor

44 **These foods are toxic to your dog.**

A cheese and broccoli

B chocolate and onions

C bread and butter

D potato chips and popcorn

Help this guy keep track of the rest of his body.

C

45. patella (kneecap)
It's the little bone that floats in the front of your knee.

B

46. funny bone (back of the elbow)
Also known as the humerus bone. If you accidentally bang it, sometimes it hurts and sometimes it just feels funny.

A

47. sternum (breastbone)
It protects your heart and lungs. It's kind of important.

D

48. tibia (shinbone) ⟶
If someone's bugging you, tell 'em you'll kick them in the tibia.

Help!

This guy lost his cranium (head).

Help him keep track of the rest of his body.

A

B

C

D

45
Where is his *patella*?

46
Where is his *funny bone*?

47
Where is his *sternum*?

48
Where is his *tibia*?

49. *If you attended a fancy dinner in ancient Egypt, your waiter might have been...*

A BABOON

D

Baboons would carry the food to your table in pouches inside their cheeks. Which is probably why there aren't too many ancient Egyptian restaurants in your neighborhood.

TONIGHT'S SPECIAL IS THE GRILLED GAZELLE. I HUNTED IT MYSELF.

---

50. *The greatest period of pirate activity was from the 16th century to the 18th century. Why did pirates in that era wear earrings?*

TO IMPROVE THEIR EYESIGHT

B

It is during this time that travel on trade routes to the East became more common, and pirates were introduced to the practice of acupuncture. It was widely believed that piercing one's body with metal improved eyesight.

---

51. *Cave people used to eat...*

ROOTS AND BERRIES

D

Dinosaurs did not exist alongside prehistoric cave people, nor did cheetahs or cheese. Roots and berries, on the other hand, have been around for a long time.

---

52. *What did women in Elizabethan England do to get rid of wrinkles?*

SLEPT WITH STRIPS OF RAW MEAT ON THEIR FACES

C

It was beef for beauty. It also worked well as perfume if you were trying to attract a really hungry man. Incidentally, the ancient Egyptians used crushed tadpoles to make a hair dye.

---

53. *You're the leader of one team playing in the big Mayan ball game in the city of Uxmal about 1,100 years ago. Why do you really want to win?*

IF YOUR TEAM LOSES, YOU'LL GET YOUR HEAD CUT OFF.

D

Let's see some hustle out there.

GOOD GAME!

49 If you attended a fancy dinner in ancient **Egypt**, your waiter might have been...

A a mummy

C an out-of-work actor

B an elephant

D a baboon

50 The greatest period of pirate activity was from the 16th century to the 18th century. Why did pirates in that era wear earrings?

A to give them a place to hang their keys

C to prevent seasickness

B to improve their eyesight

D to show their rank on the ship

HISTORY

51 Cave people used to eat...

A dinosaurs

B fast food (like cheetahs)

C cheese

D roots and berries

52 What did women in Elizabethan England do to get rid of wrinkles?

A used Botox

C slept with strips of raw meat on their faces

B smeared their cheeks with chicken fat

D applied a paste made from crushed tadpoles

53 You're the leader of one team playing in the big Mayan ball game in the city of Uxmal about 1,100 years ago. Why do you really want to win?

A There's a banquet for the winning team.

C You might get a fifty-million-peso sandal deal.

B The winner gets to go to the Mexican Nationals.

D If your team loses, you'll get your head cut off.

54. Your mother's father's name is Funky. What do you call him?

Grandfather Funky

If he was a priest you could call him Father Grandfather
Funky. Or maybe just Father Funky?

55. What do you call your cousin's kid?

my second cousin

Can you name a real one of yours?

56. Your father's brother's son is your...

cousin

Your father's brother is your uncle.
His kids are your cousins.

57. Your sister has a baby girl. How is that baby girl related to you?

She's your niece.

If your sister had a boy, that would be your nephew.

*58. Brainless is your father's father's brother. He's having
a birthday and you have to buy him a card. What should it say?*

Happy Birthday Great-Uncle Brainless

He is your father's uncle. To you he is known as
a great-uncle. And a pretty good cook.

54 **Your mother's father's name is Funky. What do you call him?**

A Uncle Funky

C Grandfather Funky

B Great-Grandfather Funky

D Cousin Funky

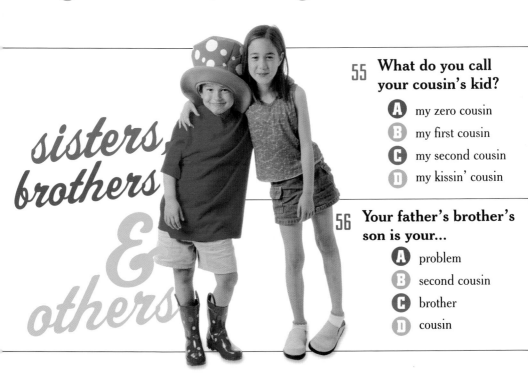

sisters,
brothers
&
others

55 **What do you call your cousin's kid?**

A my zero cousin

B my first cousin

C my second cousin

D my kissin' cousin

56 **Your father's brother's son is your...**

A problem

B second cousin

C brother

D cousin

57 **Your sister has a baby girl. How is that baby girl related to you?**

A She's your niece.

C You're her babysitter.

B She's your nephew.

D She's your stepsister.

58 **Brainless is your father's father's brother. He's having a birthday, and you have to buy him a card. What should it say?**

A Happy Birthday Great-Uncle Brainless

C Happy Birthday Brother Brainless

B Happy Birthday Uncle Brainless

D Merry Christmas Tony!

59. You can drink milk from a cow and which other mammal?

all of the above

Being able to produce milk is what makes a mammal a mammal. A reptile cannot make milk. That's why no one ever asks for a tall glass of lizard milk.

D

60. Although you only have one, a cow has four…

stomachs

That's why a cow eats all day. It takes her forever to get full.

B

61. In one year, a 1,000-pound cow creates 10 tons of…

manure

Think about this before you tell your parents you want a cow for your birthday. You'll need a big shovel.

B

62. Cows are known to spend a lot of time chewing their "cud." What is cud?

semi-digested food they spit up into their mouths

They actually regurgitate food from their first stomach into their mouths. Can you say "breath mint"?

C

63. Cows are a big source of…

methane

Methane gas is a big part of pollution. (Hey! You try eating all that grass without creating a "social problem.")

A

59 You can drink milk from a cow and which other mammal?

A yak

C sheep

B goat

D all of the above

let's talk
COWS

LET'S!

60 Although you only have one, a cow has four...

A chins

B stomachs

C wheel drive

D livers

61 In one year, a 1,000-pound cow creates 10 tons of...

A beef

B manure

C milk

D eggs

62 Cows are known to spend a lot of time chewing their "cud." What is cud?

A another name for their tongue

C semi-digested food they spit up into their mouths

B a brand of cow bubble gum

D a type of flower that grows in fields

63 Cows are a big source of...

A methane

C mutton

B tofu

D venison

64. One of the main ingredients for making glass is sand.

Way!

Heating sand to a really high temperature creates glass.
A lightning strike on the beach will leave glass lumps.

65. Reading in dim light is bad for your eyes.

No way!

You may get a headache because you're straining
your eyes. But you won't do any permanent damage.

66. Egyptian mummy-makers got rid of the brains by fishing them out with hooks through the noses.

Way!

Mummy brains did come out through their noses.
(Brains were considered unimportant.)

67. Texas Governor James Hogg (1851-1906) named his only daughter "Ima."

Way!

Ima Hogg (who never married) was a prominent
Houston philanthropist who died in 1975.

68. Eskimos have more than 30 words for snow.

No Way!

Contrary to what you may have heard,
Eskimos have only three or four
words for snow.

64 One of the main ingredients for making glass is sand.

    A Way!   **B** No way!

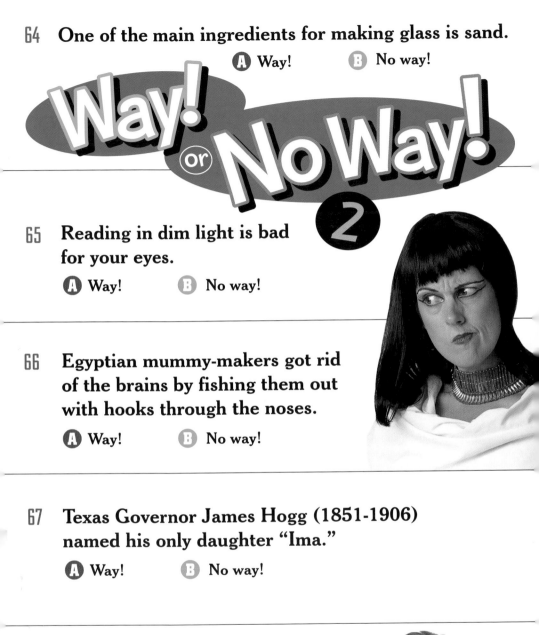

Way! or No Way! 2

65 Reading in dim light is bad for your eyes.

    A Way!   **B** No way!

66 Egyptian mummy-makers got rid of the brains by fishing them out with hooks through the noses.

    A Way!   **B** No way!

67 Texas Governor James Hogg (1851-1906) named his only daughter "Ima."

    A Way!   **B** No way!

68 Eskimos have more than 30 words for snow.

    A Way!   **B** No way!

69. Which of these shapes is a pentagon?

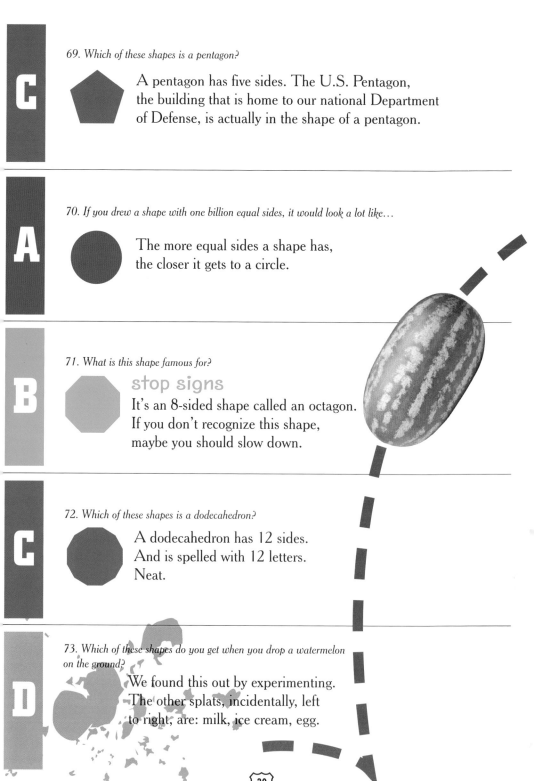

C

A pentagon has five sides. The U.S. Pentagon, the building that is home to our national Department of Defense, is actually in the shape of a pentagon.

70. If you drew a shape with one billion equal sides, it would look a lot like...

A

The more equal sides a shape has, the closer it gets to a circle.

71. What is this shape famous for?

B

stop signs

It's an 8-sided shape called an octagon. If you don't recognize this shape, maybe you should slow down.

72. Which of these shapes is a dodecahedron?

C

A dodecahedron has 12 sides. And is spelled with 12 letters. Neat.

73. Which of these shapes do you get when you drop a watermelon on the ground?

D

We found this out by experimenting. The other splats, incidentally, left to right, are: milk, ice cream, egg.

69 Which of these shapes is a *pentagon*?

A B C D

70 If you drew a shape with one billion equal sides, it would look a lot like...

A B C D

71 What is this shape famous for?

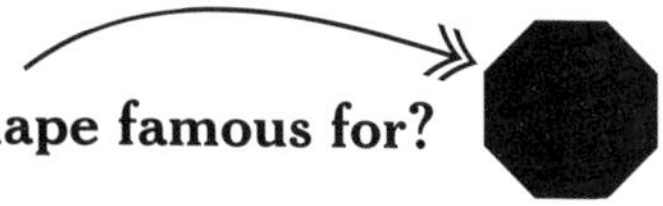

A robot foot prints **C** freckles

B stop signs **D** All snowflakes look like it.

Good Shape

72 Which of these shapes is a *dodecahedron*?

A B C D

73 Which of these shapes do you get when you drop a watermelon on the ground?

A B C D

C

74. A giraffe's legs are 6 feet long.
How do you think Mom delivers her babies?

standing up

A baby giraffe's introduction to the world is a 6-foot drop.
Waaaaaaaaaaaah!

B

75. In your first year of life, what happens?

Your weight triples.

Keep that pace up and you'll weigh more
than 11 million pounds by age 13.

D

76. How big would a group of bacteria this size • grow to be
in three days (assuming ideal conditions)?

planet Earth

Bacteria breed like crazy. They outrun their
food supply very quickly.

A

77. When you were just born...

You had a soft spot
in your head.

Your vision was blurry, but you weren't blind.
And that soft spot closed up when you were
nine to eighteen months old.

A

78. When you are 4 feet 3 inches, you are as tall as...

Shaquille O'Neal's belly button

You can try to block his shot from down there.
Or just tie his shoelaces together.

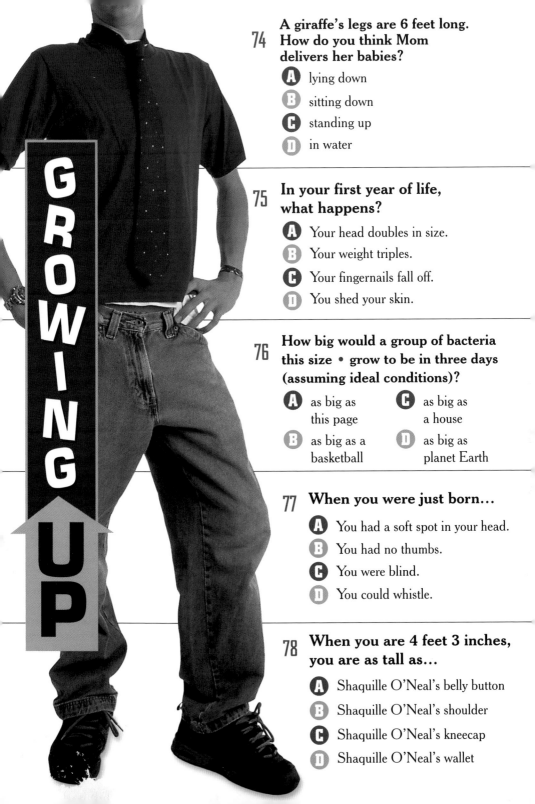

GROWING UP

74 A giraffe's legs are 6 feet long. How do you think Mom delivers her babies?

A lying down

B sitting down

C standing up

D in water

75 In your first year of life, what happens?

A Your head doubles in size.

B Your weight triples.

C Your fingernails fall off.

D You shed your skin.

76 How big would a group of bacteria this size • grow to be in three days (assuming ideal conditions)?

A as big as this page

B as big as a basketball

C as big as a house

D as big as planet Earth

77 When you were just born...

A You had a soft spot in your head.

B You had no thumbs.

C You were blind.

D You could whistle.

78 When you are 4 feet 3 inches, you are as tall as...

A Shaquille O'Neal's belly button

B Shaquille O'Neal's shoulder

C Shaquille O'Neal's kneecap

D Shaquille O'Neal's wallet

79. *It is said that orangutans have four of these, but you have only two. What is it?*

hands

Their feet have thumbs on the side like your hands, rather than a big toe next to the other toes. This makes orangutans excellent tree climbers.

---

80. *The monkey that is most like a human is...*

the chimpanzee

Humans and chimps share more than 98% of the same DNA. They are almost human. Or **we** are almost monkey. Scary.

---

81. *A mature male gorilla is also called...*

a silverback

At around age 10–12, the mature males get gray hair on their backs. In humans, that happens a little later. At least it should.

---

82. *Why are spider monkeys called spider monkeys?*

They look like spiders because of their long tails.

They have long legs and long tails. And they use their tail like another leg. They can grab things and hang from it. The Spiderman of the jungle.

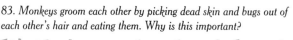

---

83. *Monkeys groom each other by picking dead skin and bugs out of each other's hair and eating them. Why is this important?*

It's their number 1 social activity.

It's what they do to bond with each other. So, next time you're hanging out with a friend, show them you care. Eat a bug out of their hair.

79 It is said that *orangutans* have four of these, but you have only two. What is it?

A ears

C buttocks

B eyes

D hands

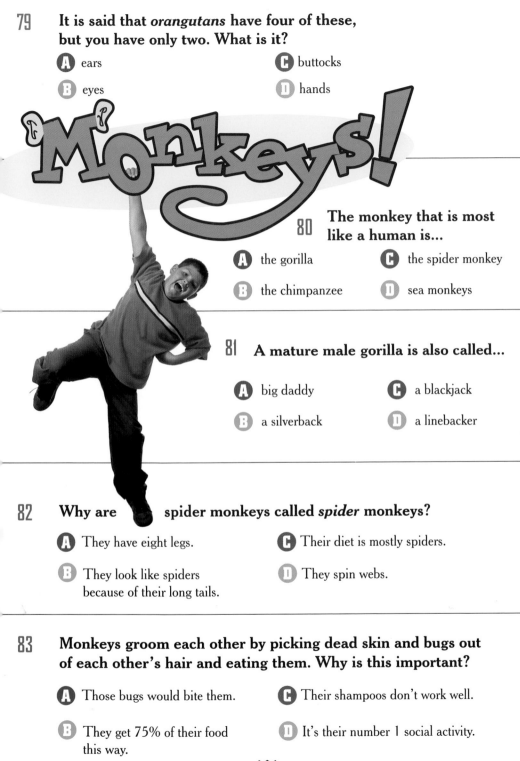

Monkeys!

80 The monkey that is most like a human is...

A the gorilla

C the spider monkey

B the chimpanzee

D sea monkeys

81 A mature male gorilla is also called...

A big daddy

C a blackjack

B a silverback

D a linebacker

82 Why are spider monkeys called *spider* monkeys?

A They have eight legs.

C Their diet is mostly spiders.

B They look like spiders because of their long tails.

D They spin webs.

83 Monkeys groom each other by picking dead skin and bugs out of each other's hair and eating them. Why is this important?

A Those bugs would bite them.

C Their shampoos don't work well.

B They get 75% of their food this way.

D It's their number 1 social activity.

84. *British merchants began importing something from India beginning around 1653 that quickly became enormously popular. The population of England, in fact, became semi-addicted to the stuff. It is...*

tea

One of the "plants that changed history." Tea's active ingredient is caffeine, which took Europe by storm when it was first introduced.

85. *In the late 1990s, a news and weather show broadcast in Russia became very popular when...*

The reporters began doing the show naked.

The anchors on *The Naked Truth*, who reported the news just as if they were wearing clothes, became a nationwide sensation.

86. *Ice skating is a hugely popular sport in...*

Holland

Holland is in the Netherlands, a part of Europe with cold winters. It's as far north as Canada and ice skating is almost the national sport.

87. *About how old was Tutankhamen, a famous Egyptian pharaoh, when construction began on his tomb?*

just born

Pharoahs were buried in pyramids that could take as many as 20 years to build. Since early deaths were not uncommon, one of the first things done upon the birth of a new pharaoh was to get ready for his death.

88. *Who was the first to call the natives of North America "Indians"?*

Christopher Columbus

Christopher Columbus called the natives Indians because he believed he had sailed all the way to India on his voyage in 1492. He was wrong, actually, by about half a planet. The name is a mistake that stuck.

84 British merchants began importing something from India beginning around 1653 that quickly became enormously popular. The population of England, in fact, became semi-addicted to the stuff. It is...

A spice

C tea

B coffee

D opium

---

85 In the late 1990s, a news and weather show broadcast in Russia became very popular when...

A The reporters began doing the show naked.

C The reporters routinely punched and bit each other.

B A trained monkey was used as the main reporter.

D The news stories were always sung to rock music.

---

86 Ice skating is a hugely popular sport in...

A The Ivory Coast

C Australia

B Holland

D Venezuela

---

87 About how old was Tutankhamen, a famous Egyptian pharaoh, when construction began on his tomb?

A 45

C 25

B 35

D just born

Around the World

---

88 Who was the first to call the natives of North America "Indians?"

A George Washington

C Thomas Jefferson

B Christopher Columbus

D Marco Polo

B

89. How many times a year does the average person use the toilet?

2,500

That time adds up. You spend about three entire years of your life on the toilet.

A

90. Who is often incorrectly credited with inventing the flushable toilet?

Thomas Crapper

That was his real name. He was an English inventor in the plumbing world in the mid-to-late 1800s. However, most research indicates it was actually invented by his employee, Albert Giblin.

D

91. Before the invention of toilet paper, what did people use?

all of these

When in need, you'll make do with what's close by. People also used snow, lace and even newspaper.

C

92. Most toilet paper is perforated. What does that mean?

It's pre-punched.

It's pre-cut to tear off in neat little square sheets.

D

93. How many bathrooms are in the White House?

more than 30

The White House has 132 rooms, and 35 of those are bathrooms. Which, because of the shape of the toilet, could also be considered Oval Offices.

89 How many times a year does the average person use the toilet?

A 1,500

C 500

B 2,500

D twice

90 Who is often incorrectly credited with inventing the flushable toilet?

A Thomas Crapper

C John Johnson

B Michael Charmin

D Peter Flushing

91 Before the invention of toilet paper, what did people use?

A sheep's wool

C book pages

B corn cobs

D all of these

92 Most toilet paper is *perforated*. What does that mean?

A It's scented.

C It's pre-punched.

B It's cheap.

D It's recycled.

93 How many bathrooms are in the White House?

A 11

C 27

B 18

D more than 30

94. On an average day, how long does a cat sleep?

17 hours

But their senses remain very active. It's almost impossible to sneak up on a sleeping cat. Unlike some humans who can sleep through anything.

C

95. Cats have five toes on their front paws, but how many toes on their back feet?

four

That's why most cats, as smart as they seem, can count only to 18.

A

96. A group of kittens is called...

a kindle

A group of puppies is called a litter.

D

ALL THIS TIME
I THOUGHT I WAS
ONE OF A KIND.
I WAS JUST ONE
OF A KINDLE.

97. Most cats have no...

eyelashes

So when you're buying make-up
for your kitty, no mascara.
In fact, lipstick may be
a bad idea as well.

C

98. What do cats use their whiskers for?

for balance

They use them as sensors to feel what's around them. They are very sensitive and can even feel changes in air pressure. If you cut your cat's whiskers, it would have a tough time getting around.

B

94 On an average day, how long does a cat sleep?

A 8 hours

C 17 hours

B 12 hours

D all day

95 Cats have five toes on their front paws, but how many toes on their back feet?

A four

C six

B five

D three

96 A group of kittens is called...

A a cuddle

C a gaggle

B a puddle

D a kindle

97 Most cats have no...

A ears

C eyelashes

B livers

D common sense

98 What do cats use their whiskers for?

A to taste their food

C to stay warm

B for balance

D to look older

99. *When a tree is knocked down or chopped down, how can you tell how old it was?*

BY COUNTING THE RINGS IN ITS TRUNK

Each ring in a tree's trunk shows one growing season.

100. *Trees provide this for all of us.*

ALL OF THESE

You can see the shade and the wood.
But trees feed oxygen into the atmosphere.
The rain forest is sometimes called
the lungs of the planet.

THANKS FOR THE SHADES.

101. *The tallest trees in the world are...*

REDWOODS

They can grow over 360 feet in the air.
(That's a football field plus some.)

102. *The oldest trees in the world are...*

PINES

There are bristlecone pines that are more than 4,000 years old.
We kid you knot.

103. *The only type of tree that can become a Christmas tree is an evergreen tree. What's that mean?*

IT DOESN'T LOSE ITS NEEDLES IN THE WINTER.

The other type of tree is called deciduous. That's the kind of tree
that loses its leaves in the fall and winter.

99 When a tree is knocked down or chopped down, how can you tell how old it was?

A by counting the rings in its trunk

B by tasting the sap

C by measuring the diameter of the trunk

D by asking the squirrels

100 Trees provide this for all of us.

A shade

B oxygen

C wood

D all of these

MR. TREE, MAY I ASK YOU A FEW QUESTIONS?

I WISH YOU WOOD.

101 The tallest trees in the world are...

A spruces

B oaks

C redwoods

D pines

102 The oldest trees in the world are...

A spruces

B oaks

C pines

D redwoods

103 The only type of tree that can become a Christmas tree is an evergreen tree. What's that mean?

A It doesn't lose its needles in the winter.

B It's fireproof.

C It's stain-resistant.

D It's small enough to fit in your house.

43

B

104. What are Hansel and Gretel famous for?

finding a house made of cakes and sugar

They stop to eat the house. Then out of the house comes a witch who puts Hansel in a cage. Then they escape and push the witch into the fire and run home. What a day.

A

105. What happens to Little Red Riding Hood?

The wolf eats her for dinner.

You'll be relieved to hear she came out all right by the end of the story.

C

106. When Little Red Riding Hood grew up, she probably became…

a pizza delivery person

Our first choice is pizza delivery person, just because she seems to enjoy bringing people food, although some folks would argue she was headed for animal dentistry because of her interest in wolf teeth. So we'll accept B, too.

SORRY QUEEN, BUT THAT SNOW WHITE IS A HOTTIE!

B

107. The queen thought she was "the fairest of them all." Who told her that "Snow White is fairer than you"?

her mirror

The truth hurts.

A

108. Goldilocks broke into the three bears' house and ate some of their porridge. What's porridge?

soft oatmeal boiled in milk

Yuck. She should have made herself some French toast.

Hansel and Gretel

did what?

and other fairy tale trivia

104 **What are Hansel and Gretel famous for?**

A fetching a pail of water

B finding a house made of cakes and sugar

C sticking their thumbs in pies

D playing doubles tennis

105 **What happens to Little Red Riding Hood?**

A The wolf eats her for dinner.

B Her grandmother won't let her in.

C She conks the wolf on the head.

D She gets lost in the woods.

106 **When Little Red Riding Hood grew up, she probably became**

A an animal rights activist

B a dentist for animals

C a pizza delivery person

D the voice of Darth Vader

107 **The queen thought she was "the fairest of them all." Who told her that "Snow White is fairer than you"?**

A a little birdie

B her mirror

C her wicked stepsisters

D Ricky, the guy who cleans the pool

108 **Goldilocks broke into the three bears' house and ate some of their porridge. What's *porridge*?**

A soft oatmeal boiled in milk

B a bowl of beef

C bear chow from a bag

D a mix of eggs and cheeses

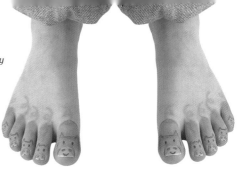

B

109. Pigs are the only animal that has to worry about this human problem.

sunburn

That's why you don't see any pigs at the beach.

C

110. Some people like to race pigs. But there are some who think that it's cruel to the pig. Why?

They have no sweat glands.

So when someone is really hot and says "I'm sweating like a pig," they don't know what they're talking about. They could say, "I'm sweating like a horse."

A

111. What do pigs eat to help them digest food?

dirt

Usually that's all that's left when they're done with dinner.

B

112. Pigs are among the top 10 of these animals...

smartest

They're right up there with dolphins, dogs and cats. You can train a pig to herd sheep. And even to act. (Which a pig did in *Babe*.)

A

113. This is true about pigs around the world.

They are the most commonly eaten animal.

Yes, people think they are very smart. But they also think that they're tasty.

109 Pigs are the only animal that has to worry about this human problem.

A double vision

C headaches

B sunburn

D flossing

---

110 Some people like to race pigs. But there are some who think that it's cruel to the pig. Why?

A They're not competitive.

C They have no sweat glands.

B They're terribly slow.

D They have no knees.

---

111 What do pigs eat to help them digest food?

A dirt   **B** milkshakes   **C** wood   **D** grubs

112 Pigs are among the top 10 of these animals...

A dumbest   **B** smartest   **C** biggest   **D** stinkiest

---

113 This is true about pigs around the world.

A They are the most commonly eaten animal.

C They cause the most disease.

B They are the most hated.

D They are the number 1 pet for the home.

A

114. What are you scared of if you have claustrophobia?

confined spaces

When you turn 16, you may not want a car. They're so small. You can just walk for the rest of your life.

C

115. What are you scared of if you have phonophobia?

your own voice

Do not read this answer aloud.

B

116. What are you afraid of if you have trichophobia?

hair

Don't look now — there's one sitting on your head.

D

117. What are you afraid of if you have scolionophobia?

school

There is a cure for this. It's called graduation.

Noooooooooo!

D

118. What are you afraid of if you have panophobia?

everything

Good luck.

What are you scared of?

114 What are you scared of if you have *claustrophobia*?

- **A** confined spaces
- **C** clothes
- **B** wide open spaces
- **D** Santa

115 What are you scared of if you have *phonophobia*?

- **A** the phone
- **C** your own voice
- **B** record players
- **D** fakes

116 What are you scared of if you have *trichophobia*?

- **A** magicians
- **C** clocks
- **B** hair
- **D** sneezing

117 What are you scared of if you have *scolionophobia*?

- **A** spelling
- **C** lions
- **B** cold weather
- **D** school

118 What are you scared of if you have *panophobia*?

- **A** frying pans
- **C** flutes
- **B** pain
- **D** everything

A

119. A Frenchman who performs under the name Monsieur Mangetout (Mr. Eats Everything) once ate a grocery cart.

Way!

He has also eaten a bicycle. Apparently, bananas and hard-boiled eggs make him ill.

B

120. 40% of your body weight is brains.

No way!

If you thought you were 40% brains, you're probably 80% ego. The average adult human brain weighs in at around 3 pounds.

A

121. Breakfast cereals all contain a small fraction of insect body parts. How big a fraction is set by law.

Way!

Your Chocolate Swirl Cluster Puffs are no exception — but the parts usually do not exceed 4 or 5 millimeters in length. Crunchy.

B

122. If you dropped a penny off the Empire State Building, it would burn through the hand of anyone who tried to catch it.

No way!

Pennies fall more like feathers than rocks. Besides, many pennies never even reach the ground. They fall onto roofs of adjacent buildings.

B

123. The turtle is the world's slowest land animal.

No way!

The big slowpoke is the snail.

FORGET THE HARE, LET'S RACE A SNAIL.

GOOD IDEA.

119 A Frenchman who performs under the name Monsieur Mangetout (Mr. Eats Everything) once ate a grocery cart.

A Way!　　**B** No way!

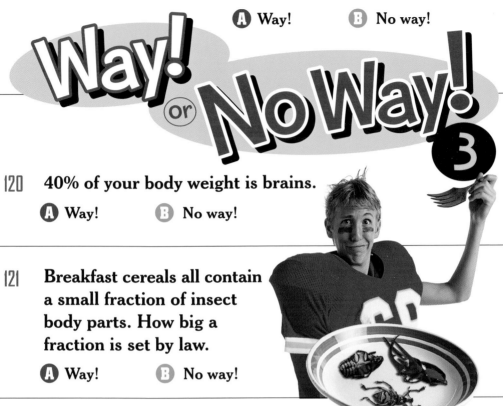

120 40% of your body weight is brains.

A Way!　　**B** No way!

121 Breakfast cereals all contain a small fraction of insect body parts. How big a fraction is set by law.

A Way!　　**B** No way!

122 If you dropped a penny off the Empire State Building, it would burn through the hand of anyone who tried to catch it.

A Way!

B No way!

123 The turtle is the world's slowest land animal.

A Way!　　**B** No way!

B

124. *Where would I find your larynx?*

in your throat

Your vocal cords are in your larynx.

C

125. *Where would I find your philtrum?*

on your face

It's that funny little notch
between your nose and your mouth.

A

126. *Where would I find your vertebrae?*

in your back

They're all the bones that make up your spine.

C

127. *Where would I find your aglet?*

on your shoe

An aglet is the metal or plastic tip on the end of your shoelace.

B

128. *Where would I find your love line?*

in your hand

When a psychic reads your palm, they look
at the lines, and one of them is your "love line."

124 **Where would I find your larynx?**

   A in your eyes   **C** in your backpack

   B in your throat   **D** in your hair

125 **Where would I find your philtrum?**

   A on your leg   **C** on your face

   B next to your stomach   **D** in your bedroom

126 **Where would I find your vertebrae?**

   A in your back   **C** in a pasta shop

   B in your legs   **D** in your ears

127 **Where would I find your aglet?**

   A under your bed   **C** on your shoe

   B in your throat   **D** between your toes

128 **Where would I find your love line?**

   A in your heart   **C** on the roof of your mouth

   B in your hand   **D** in your bathroom

It's all about you

OF COURSE

A

129. Pumpkins are fruits.

They belong in the fruits food group.
And on your porch on Halloween.

B

130. Eggs are protein.

And they're great for breakfast.

D

131. Tomatoes are fruits.

People often think they are a vegetable.
Trick question: A fruit has its seeds on the inside
(apples, peaches). A vegetable does not (celery).

B

132. Donuts are all fats and sugars.

Fats and sugars are also known as
the really yummy food group.

A

133. Cheese is dairy.

These are foods that come from milk.

PUTTING FOOD WHERE IT BELONGS

other than in your mouth

129

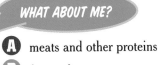

I'M LOST! WHAT FOOD GROUP CAN I CALL HOME?

A fruits
B vegetables
C cereals and grains
D bad seeds

WHAT ABOUT US?

A fruits
B meats and other proteins
C dairy
D food for eggheads

130

WHERE DO I GO?

A vegetables
B meats and other proteins
C fun-to-smash food
D fruits

131

WHAT ABOUT ME?

A meats and other proteins
B fats and sugars
C dairy
D things that are round

132

I'M WITH THIS GROUP.

A dairy
B meats and other proteins
C fats and sugars
D mouse chow

133

C

134. *If you could jump as well as a flea can, proportionately, what's the biggest thing you could jump over?*

A SKYSCRAPER

The tiny flea can jump about 13 inches. If a flea were your size, it could clear 80-story skyscrapers with ease.

B

135. *How do flies taste?*

THROUGH THEIR FEET

That fly walking across your birthday cake is just tasting the frosting.

A

136. *It's mosquito season! Which dessert is a really bad call?*

A BANANA SPLIT

The Canadian National Park Service advises visitors that if they eat bananas, their skin will produce a smell that is very attractive to skeeters.

C

137. *How do grasshoppers make that singing noise?*

THEY RUB THEIR LEGS AND WINGS TOGETHER.

And they make it look so easy.

D

138. *Totally gross but true: One kind of bedbug…*

BARKS WHEN IT SMELLS HUMAN FLESH

Wait, it gets even weirder: The U.S. Army once tried to use these bedbugs to locate hidden enemy soldiers. They made tiny capsules that contained bedbugs and tiny radio transmitters. The plan was to drop these on supposed hideouts and listen for tiny barks. We are not making this up!

134 **If you could jump as well as a flea can, proportionately, what's the biggest thing you could jump over?**

Ⓐ a garbage can

Ⓒ a skyscraper

Ⓑ a flagpole

Ⓓ the moon

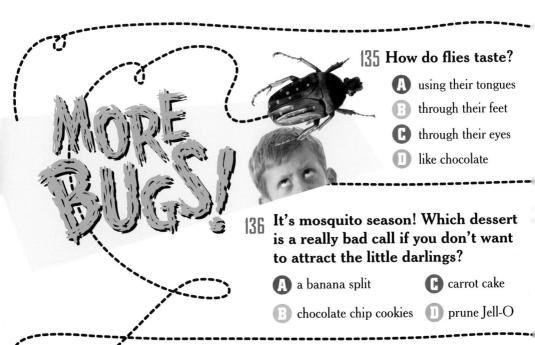

135 How do flies taste?

Ⓐ using their tongues

Ⓑ through their feet

Ⓒ through their eyes

Ⓓ like chocolate

136 **It's mosquito season! Which dessert is a really bad call if you don't want to attract the little darlings?**

Ⓐ a banana split

Ⓒ carrot cake

Ⓑ chocolate chip cookies

Ⓓ prune Jell-O

137 **How do grasshoppers make that singing noise?**

Ⓐ They whistle through their little lips.

Ⓒ They rub their legs and wings together.

Ⓑ They spin their heads really fast.

Ⓓ They yodel while doing the polka.

138 **Totally gross but true: One kind of bedbug...**

Ⓐ looks just like popcorn, before and after it gets popped

Ⓒ sucks blood until it looks like a little tomato

Ⓑ climbs inside nostrils and eats boogers

Ⓓ barks when it smells human flesh

C

139. *One of these phrases is an example of alliteration. Which one?*

BOOGIE BUBBLE BOOTIES

Alliteration is the repetition of the same consonant sounds. This phrase gives you the triple B-B-B sound.

D

140. *Which word here is often a verb?*

VOMIT

Verbs are action words. If you had hundreds of millions of cookies you would be forced into an action word. You would vomit.

C

141. *Which word here is an adjective?*

PURPLE

Adjectives describe things. If you ate a *pickle* (noun), you'd *pucker* up (verb) and turn *purple* (adjective).

D

142. *Which word here is a noun?*

MONKEY

A noun is a person, place or thing. In this list the monkey is the thing. Or is it a person?

D

143. *Which of these words is an example of onomatopoeia?*

ALL OF THESE

These are all words that imitate the sound of something.

139 One of these phrases is an example of *alliteration*. Which one?

A boogie disco bumpy

C boogie bubble booties

B Snookie Pango McGoo

D dandy flank snacks

The exciting, amazing, action-packed world of LANGUAGE

140 Which word here is often a *verb*?

A hundreds **B** millions **C** cookies **D** vomit

141 Which word here is an *adjective*?

A pickles

C purple

B prunes

D pucker

142 Which word here is a *noun*?

A very

C chunky

B ugly

D monkey

143 Which of these words is an example of *onomatopoeia*?

A

B

C

D all of these

D

144. Bart first looked a little...

ochre

It's a type of yellow to yellow-orange color.

A

145. Then his face went a little...

crimson

It's a vivid red. The football team from the University of Alabama is known as "the Crimson Tide." They wear red.

B

146. Then he went completely...

indigo

It's a deep blue.

C

147. Then it got really freaky when his face went...

olive

Okay, this one was easy. Olives are olive colored. Green. Unless they are black olives. Who knows what color those are?

A

148. Another word to describe how Bart was feeling after his fish is...

nauseated

It means feeling sick to your stomach. Which can happen if you get food poisoning. It's no fun.

Bart just ate a bad piece of fish. He doesn't look so good. What color describes Bart?

144
Bart first looked a little ochre.

145
Then his face went a little crimson.

146
Then he went completely indigo.

147
Then it really got freaky when his face went olive.

148 Another word to describe how Bart was feeling after his fish is...

A nauseated

C giddy

B splendiferous

D romantic

B

149. Which of these is true about sharks?

We kill lots more of them than they do of us.

Sharks rarely attack people. People, on the other hand, kill and eat thousands of sharks every year.

A

150. Which of these is an actual delicacy in China?

shark fin soup

We hear it tastes just like chicken.

D

151. The biggest breed of shark is...

whale shark

A whale shark can reach lengths of up to 50 feet. The smallest shark is called the spined pygmy shark, and it's small enough to fit in your hand. How cute.

D

152. How many bones does an adult shark have?

None

Sharks are boneless. Their "skeleton" is made of cartilage. Just like your ears and nose.

B

153. Why is a shark's belly lighter in color than its back?

to better camouflage itself

It's called countershading. Their backs are dark, so it's harder to see them from the water surface. And their bellies are lighter so as to blend with the surface better.

149 **Which of these is true about sharks?**

A They're the most dangerous animals on Earth.

B We kill lots more of them than they do of us.

C Sometimes they slither up onto the beach and eat sunbathers.

D They have the same set of teeth for life.

150 **Which of these is an actual delicacy in China?**

A shark fin soup

B shark snout sandwiches

C shark tooth ice cream

D shark eyeball burritos

SHARKS!

151 **The biggest breed of shark is...**

A great white

B hammerhead

C Sharkquille O'Neal

D whale shark

152 **How many bones does an adult shark have?**

A 125

B 18

C 59

D none

153 **Why is a shark's belly lighter in color than its back?**

A Its back is sunburned.

B to better camouflage itself

C It has two different layers of skin.

D It brings out the blue in its eyes.

*154. Let's play that game where we all make a chain
and then run around like crazy. What's it called again?*

Crack the Whip

American artist Winslow Homer (1836-1910)
did a great painting of kids playing Crack the Whip.

155. Which of these games goes back the farthest?

chess

Chess was the first to appear on the scene, although
Candyland was probably the first board game
you ever played.

156. Which of these is most similar to the game Sardines?

Hide and Go Seek

Sardines is the version where you join the hider
in their hiding place.

*157. Name the game where you attempt to attach an appendage
to a picture of an animal.*

Pin the Tail on the Donkey

And it's not for sissies. Any game combining
dizzy kids, blindfolds and sharp points
should be classified as "extreme."

*158. Let's play that game where we all sit in a circle
and a message is whispered from ear to ear.*

Telephone

That's the game where the message goes from
"I brought the big box" to "I loved the pig's socks."

154 Let's play that game where we all make a chain and then run around like crazy. What's it called again?

A Chain Gang   **C** Statues

B Crack the Whip   **D** Mother May I

155 Which of these games goes back the farthest?

A Monopoly   **C** Scrabble

B Chess   **D** Candyland

LET'S PLAY...

NAME THAT GAME

156 Which of these is most similar to the game Sardines?

A Freeze Tag   **C** Marco Polo

B Hide and Go Seek   **D** Capture the Flag

157 Name the game where you attempt to attach an appendage to a picture of an animal.

A Ride 'em Cowboy   **C** Pigs in a Pen

B Pin the Tail on the Donkey   **D** Duck Duck Goose

158 Let's play that game where we all sit in a circle and a message is whispered from ear to ear.

A I Spy   **C** Telephone

B Gossip   **D** Mumblety-Peg

B

159. What does the female praying mantis do after mating?

bites the head off her mate

Which is why male praying mantises are
so often a little slow to warm up to the girls.

HEY, DON'T TAKE IT PERSONALLY.

B

160.When a goose has a baby, what do they call it?

a gosling

baby duck = duckling
baby goose = gosling
baby skunk = kit
(We don't make the rules.)

D

161. When a mule has a baby, what do they call it?

a miracle

Mules are the offspring of a horse and a donkey —
and they cannot have babies themselves.

A

162. What is the most popular pet in North America?

cat

But don't tell the other three.

I'M #1!

D

163. Which animal's baby is called a calf?

all of them

Icebergs also have calves. They're the little icebergs that calve off the big ones.

159 **What does the female praying mantis do after mating?**

A begins making a nest   **C** sheds her skin

B bites the head off her mate   **D** tells all her friends

Hairy Babies

160 **When a goose has a baby, what do they call it?**

A a goose drop   **C** a chick

B a gosling   **D** goosita

ARE YOU MY MOMMY?

161 **When a mule has a baby, what do they call it?**

A a colt   **C** a foal

B a burro   **D** a miracle

162 **What is the most popular pet in North America?**

A cat   **C** hamster

B dog   **D** tapeworm

163 **Which animal's baby is called a *calf*?**

A cow   **C** whale

B elephant   **D** all of them

164. I like warm water of the Caribbean, I bring heavy rains and high winds, and I'm such a disaster you probably give me a name. What am I?

a hurricane

These are the only natural disasters that get names like Andrew or Fran. There has yet to be a Hurricane Bubba.

165. I'm a big fan of the Midwestern U.S. In fact, I occur almost nowhere else in the entire world. I am...

a tornado

They're also known as twisters. The central U.S. plains are almost unique for tornado breeding. They occasionally strike in Australia, but other than that, they're as American as apple pie.

166. When I'm dormant, I'm just pretty. But when I'm active, it's not so pretty. I am...

a volcano

It's like a mountain that spits up magma, the hot insides of the Earth.

167. I'm under a lot of pressure, and sometimes my surface plates slip, usually just a few feet. I am...

an earthquake

The plates of the Earth's crust are straining against one another. When the strains are released, the movement is sharp and sudden. That's a quake.

168. Every year heat kills more people in North America than any other disaster. This is the second leading killer.

floods

Especially dangerous are flash floods, which happen quickly, giving no time for people to get out of the way.

164 I like the warm water of the Caribbean, I bring heavy rains and high winds, and I'm such a disaster you probably give me a name. What am I?

A a tornado

C a tidal wave

B a hurricane

D a mudslide

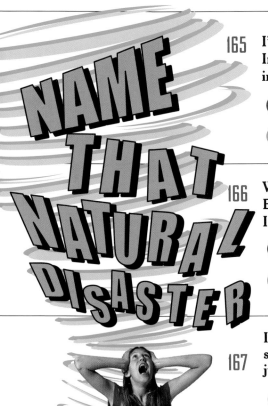

165 I'm a big fan of the Midwestern U.S. In fact, I occur almost nowhere else in the entire world. I am...

A a tornado

C a flood

B a hurricane

D a thunderstorm

166 When I'm dormant, I'm just pretty. But when I'm active, it's not pretty. I am...

A a volcano

C a tsunami

B lightning

D a tornado

167 I'm under a lot of pressure, and sometimes my surface plates slip, usually just a few feet. I am...

A a flash flood

C a blizzard

B a sonic boom

D an earthquake

168 Every year heat kills more people in North America than any other disaster. This is the second leading killer.

A earthquakes

C hurricanes

B floods

D re-runs

A

169. When a kid turns 13 years and 8 months old, what's special about that?

They celebrate their 5,000ᵀᴴ day of being alive.

And they probably don't look a day over 4,578.

B

170. One million seconds ago...

It was 11 days ago.

Where did all that time go?

C

171. One billion seconds ago...

It was 30 years ago.

Your heart beats about once per second. So your heart beats a million times in 11 days and a billion times in 30 years.

D

172. When you're way out in center field, and you see the batter hit the ball before you hear it, that's because:

The speed of light is faster than the speed of sound.

The speed of light is way, way faster than the speed of sound. So the light gets to your eyes before the sound gets to your ears.

D

173. If you had to wait a certain amount of time to collect a big jackpot, which would be the worst alternative?

a millennium

Let's hope you don't have to wait for a millennium. That's a thousand years!

BUT I WANT TO BUY A PONY NOW!

169 When a kid turns 13 years and 8 months old, what's special about that?

A They celebrate their 5,000th day of being alive.

B They've grown as tall as they'll ever be.

C Their hair starts to fall out.

D They stop believing in Santa Claus.

MATTERS OF TIME

170 One million seconds ago...

A It was yesterday.

B It was 11 days ago.

C It was 30 years ago.

D There were dinosaurs around.

171 One billion seconds ago...

A It was yesterday.

B It was 11 days ago.

C It was 30 years ago.

D There were dinosaurs around.

172 When you're way out in center field, and you see the batter hit the ball before you hear it, that's because...

A Your eyes are faster than your ears.

B The ball travels faster than sound.

C It's a hearing illusion.

D The speed of light is faster than the speed of sound.

173 If you had to wait a certain amount of time to collect a big jackpot, which would be the worst alternative?

A a month

B a century

C a decade

D a millennium

B

174. Our favorite superhero WonderChick had a busy day. Her archenemy "reprimanded" her. What'd he do?

verbally corrected her

He said that she was a little bossy to all of the bad guys. And that she should "lighten up."

DON'T MESS WITH ME!

C

175. WonderChick responded by "discombobulating" him. (Meaning...)

confused him

She asked him to spell his name, pat his head, rub his tummy and chew gum. All at the same time. He had no chance.

A

176. Then she "flumped" him.

dropped him noisily

Then she lifted him high above her head and said, "Get the point?" He didn't. He was still trying to spell his name.

D

177. Then she "lobotomized" him.

removed the front part of his brain

That way, he instantly lost 5 useless pounds.

B

178. Then, to finish him off, she "defenestrated" him.

threw him out a window

That ought to teach him not to mess with WonderChick.

174 Our favorite superhero WonderChick had a busy day after her archenemy "reprimanded" her. What'd he do?

A gave her a parking ticket

C handcuffed her to a bridge

B verbally corrected her

D egged her cape

175 WonderChick responded by "discombobulating" him. (Meaning...)

A took out his skeleton

C confused him

B filed his nails

D made him leave the room

What did WonderChick do?

176 Then she "flumped" him.

A dropped him noisily

C gave him a lecture

B slapped him with a fish

D kicked him in the shin

177 Then she "lobotomized" him.

A published lies about him

C took a picture of him

B stole his wallet

D removed the front part of his brain

178 Then, to finish him off, she "defenestrated" him.

A put him in a circus

C sent him to jail

B threw him out a window

D apologized for the whole thing

179. Where do they get the latex used to make helium balloons?

from rubber trees

Yep! Some things really do grow on trees!

180. Balloons are often used for...

weather prediction

They can float in the air, high up in the atmosphere, to predict weather patterns.

181. It is illegal in a few places to release Mylar helium balloons. Why?

They can short out power lines.

Mylar balloons contain a thin metal coating which conducts electricity.

182. Where was helium first discovered?

the sun

In 1868, an analysis of sunlight revealed the presence of an atom entirely unknown on Earth. Scientists called it helium (after "helios," sun). It was discovered on Earth almost 27 years later.

183. This is true about hot-air ballooning.

It was the first form of human flight.

People in France were flying in hot-air balloons over 100 years before the Wright brothers first flew a plane at Kitty Hawk.

QUESTIONS THAT ARE LIGHTER THAN AIR

179 Where do they get the latex used to make balloons?

- **A** from wells in the ground
- **B** from whale droppings
- **C** from rubber trees
- **D** from the hooves of horses

180 Balloons are often used for...

- **A** spying
- **B** weather prediction
- **C** cheap traveling
- **D** express shipping

181 It is illegal in a few places to release Mylar helium balloons. Why?

- **A** The police radar guns hate them.
- **B** Birds use them as mirrors.
- **C** They can short out power lines.
- **D** They poison the air.

182 Where was helium first discovered?

- **A** Earth
- **C** Mars
- **B** the sun
- **D** the moon

183 This is true about hot-air ballooning.

- **A** It was the first form of human flight.
- **C** A hot-air balloon is cheap.
- **B** You don't need a license to fly one.
- **D** It is the most dangerous way to travel.

A

184. Rudolph, who helped pull Santa's sleigh, is famous for his…

luminescent proboscis

Luminescent proboscis means "glowing nose."

C

185. If your little sister eats a bad peanut and gets sick to her stomach, you'll want to call her…

Pediatrician

Pediatrician, a doctor who treats children.

A

186. Which of these is correct?

misspelling

"Misspell" is one of the more popularly misspelled words in the language. (The MOST common mistake? "Their" when it should be "there.")

B

187. What does a taxidermist do?

stuffs animals

Whenever you see a deer head hanging on a wall, you're looking at a post-taxidermy deer.

GULP!

D

188. I have a navel, cowlick, shin and cerebellum.

I am a kid!

A cowlick is the little whirl in your hair. Your shin is on your leg and your cerebellum is a part of your brain.

184 Rudolph, who helped pull Santa's sleigh, is famous for his...

A luminescent proboscis

C intestinal parasites

B flattened arches

D psychoneuroses

185 If your little sister eats a bad peanut and gets sick to her stomach, you'll want to call her...

A veterinarian

C pediatrician

B astrologer

D chiropractor

Another stupid vocabulary quiz!

186 Which of these is correct?

A misspelling   **B** mispeling   **C** mispelling   **D** muspelling

187 What does a taxidermist do?

A builds taxis

C drives stunt cars

B stuffs animals

D collects reptiles

188 I have a navel, cowlick, shin and cerebellum. I am a...

A   **B**   **C**   **D**

189. If you order "sushi," what do you expect to eat?

raw fish

It's actually a style of cooking with vinegar. But it's most famous for the use of raw fish and seaweed. Some people love it. Others think it tastes like raw fish and seaweed.

190. What's another name for a sandwich?

all of these

You can also find sandwiches called poor boys and grinders.

191. Which of these things will you NOT find in a hamburger?

ham

It's called "hamburger" after Hamburg, Germany, the city where it first became popular.

192. What are the main ingredients in a BLT?

bacon, lettuce and tomato

It's a famous sandwich. I suppose if you like turkey, lettuce and cucumber, you could have a TLC.

193. Häagen-Dazs is a famous brand of ice cream. What does Häagen-Dazs mean in English?

Nothing.

However, Ben and Jerry *are* real guys.

189 If you order "sushi," what do you expect to eat?

A uncooked spaghetti

B live chickens

C raw fish

D peanut butter & jellyfish

190 What's another name for a sandwich?

A sub   **C** hero

B hoagie   **D** all of these

191 Which of these things will you NOT find in a hamburger?

A beef   **C** fat

B ham   **D** gristle

192 What are the main ingredients in a BLT?

A bacon, lettuce and Tabasco   **C** baked, low-fat tootsie rolls

B bacon, lice and tomato   **D** bacon, lettuce and tomato

193 Häagen-Dazs is a famous brand of ice cream. What does Häagen-Dazs mean in English?

A happy mouth   **C** horse doo-doo

B yummy days   **D** Nothing. The manufacturer just needed a fancy-sounding name.

What's for lunch?

MILDRED

Today's teenagers are tomorrow's stars!

194. Who will win a Grammy Award?

And the winner is...**Brittany.**

The Grammy is given to musicians and singers. It's called a Grammy because the award is in the shape of a little gramophone (an early record player).

B

195. Who will win an Emmy Award?

And the winner is...**Claire.**

The Emmy goes to TV shows. The award was first called an Immy, a nickname for the image orthicon tube. (That was part of an early camera.) But they called it an Emmy because the statue looked like a lady. And Emmy is better than Immy.

C

196. Who will win a Tony Award?

And the winner is...**Annette.**

The Tony is given to stars of plays and musicals on Broadway in New York City. It's named after Antoinette Perry, who was an actress, a director and a founder of the American Theatre Wing.

A

197. Who will win an Oscar?

And the winner is...**DeeDee.**

The Oscar or Academy Award goes to movie stars. It got its name years ago when an Academy librarian, Margaret Herrick, said that the statue looked like her Uncle Oscar.

D

They may seem a little weird right now, but don't be fooled.

Today's teenagers are tomorrow's stars!

A

Annette
Will one day dance and sing on Broadway.

B

Brittany
Will one day play guitar and make record albums.

C

Claire
Will one day be on a hit TV sitcom.

D

DeeDee
Will one day be a big-time movie star.

194
Who will win a Grammy Award?

195
Who will win an Emmy Award?

196
Who will win a Tony Award?

197
And who will win an Oscar?

A

198. *Back in 1932 Amelia Earhart became the FIRST woman to do this.*

fly solo across the Atlantic Ocean

It took her 14 hours and 56 minutes to do it. Nowadays that flight takes about 6 hours. And you get to watch a movie.

C

199. *Henry Ford introduced the Model T, the FIRST popular car, on October 1, 1908. What kind of gas mileage did it get?*

25 miles per gallon

Can you believe it? That's better mileage than many cars get that are built today.

A

200. *The Wright brothers completed the FIRST ever powered flight in 1903. How long did the very first flight last?*

12 seconds

They had a few more flights that day lasting as long as 57 seconds. But when Orville kept the plane in the air for 12 whole seconds, they knew they were on to something.

C

201. *Who was the FIRST person to go over Niagara Falls in a barrel?*

Annie Edson Taylor

She did it hoping to get fame and fortune on a lecture tour. She survived. But, apparently, she was a failure as a lecturer.

B

202. *Who was the FIRST woman in Space?*

Valentina Tereshkova

In 1963 she orbited Earth 48 times.

198 Back in 1932 Amelia Earhart became the FIRST woman to do this.

A fly solo across the Atlantic Ocean

C jump over buses on a motoorcyle

B drive a race car

D fly solo across the United States

---

199 Henry Ford introduced the Model T, the FIRST popular car, on October 1, 1908. What kind of gas mileage did it get?

A 1 mile per gallon

C 25 miles per gallon

B 300 yards a gallon

D It didn't even hold a gallon of gas. Only a pint.

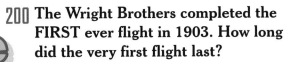

200 The Wright Brothers completed the FIRST ever flight in 1903. How long did the very first flight last?

A 12 seconds

C 30 minutes

B 1 minute

D 2 seconds

---

201 Who was the FIRST person to go over Niagara Falls in a barrel?

A Jean-Paul Durand, a 23-year-old circus acrobat

C Annie Edson Taylor, a 63-year-old teacher

B George Strauss, a 46-year-old butcher

D Anthony Peruzzi, an 18-year-old sailor

---

202 Who was the FIRST woman in Space?

A Sally Ride

C Sandra Faber

B Valentina Tereshkova

D Carla Sagan

A

203. There is dead skin in the dust in your home.

Way!

Disgusting but true. It's also true, by the way, that some of your dirt has blown in from the Sahara Desert.

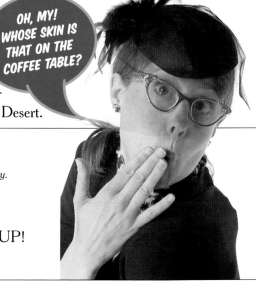

OH, MY! WHOSE SKIN IS THAT ON THE COFFEE TABLE?

B

204. Your heart beats about 1,000 times a day.

No way!

It's more like 100,000.
If you count only 1,000, WAKE UP!

B

205. Fish have eyelids like ours.

No Way!

Sharks have upper and lower eyelids, but they can't close them over their eyes. The moral: Never get into a staring contest with a shark.

B

206. There is only one word in the English language that rhymes with orange.

No way!

No words in the English language rhyme with orange. Nothing rhymes with "purple" or "silver," either.

WHAT ABOUT FLORANGE?

A

207. If you chew gum while peeling an onion, you won't cry.

Way!

It works.

84

203 There is dead skin in the dust in your home.

    A Way!   **B** No way!

Way! or No Way! 4

204 Your heart beats about 1,000 times a day.

    A Way!   **B** No way!

205
Fish have eyelids like ours.

    A Way!   **B** No way!

206 There is only one word in the English language that rhymes with orange.

    A Way!   **B** No way!

207 If you chew gum while peeling an onion, you won't cry.

    A Way!   **B** No way!

B

208. *Which of these is a rose?*

rose

A yellow rose means "friendship." A red rose means "I love you." A greenish-brown rose means "time to change the water in the vase."

A

209. *Which of these is a daisy?*

daisy

The name daisy comes from the Old English name "Day's Eye." The daisy acts like an eye, closing at night and opening in the morning. But no one has ever seen one blink.

D

210. *Which is a poinsettia?*

poinsettia

If you have dogs or little kids around, be careful where you put a poinsettia. They can be poisonous if eaten.

C

211. *And which one is a sunflower?*

sunflower

This is the only single-stemmed flower that can grow as tall as 6 feet.

D

212. *Which flower is popular at Christmas?*

poinsettia

Did the red and the green give it away?

208
Which of these is a rose?

209
Which of these is a daisy?

210
Which is a poinsettia?

211
And which one is a sunflower?

212 Which flower is popular at Christmas?

A daisy

B rose

C sunflower

D poinsettia

flower power

C

213. A baked food composed of a pastry shell filled with fruit, meat, cheese or other ingredients and usually covered with a pastry crust is...

pie

Not all pies are desserts. Pies are often filled with chicken, beef, turkey and, of course, four and twenty blackbirds.

A

214. A small, usually flat and crisp cake made from sweetened dough is...

a cookie

The number-1-selling cookie? The Oreo.

D

215. A flat, round mass of dough that is baked or fried is...

cake

So for your next birthday, instead of a cake, ask Mom to make a birthday mass of rounded dough!

B

216. A combination of selected meat trimmings ground into small pieces and pumped into a thin casing is a...

hot dog

Yummy. Delicious meat trimmings. What's a trimming?

B

217. A smooth, sweet, cold food prepared from a frozen mixture of milk products and flavorings, containing a minimum of 10% milk fat is...

ice cream

Most popular flavor? Vanilla.

213 A baked food composed of a pastry shell filled with fruit, meat, cheese or other ingredients and usually covered with a pastry crust is...

A lasagna

C pie

B pound cake

D doughnuts

they Taste better than they sound

214 A small, usually flat and crisp cake made from sweetened dough is...

A a cookie

C a brownie

B a s'more

D liver bits

215 A flat, round mass of dough that is baked or fried is...

A a waffle

C a pudding pop

B a Twinkie

D cake

216 A combination of selected meat trimmings ground into small pieces and pumped into a thin casing is...

A a hamburger

C lasagna

B a hot dog

D a meatcake

217 A smooth, sweet, cold food prepared from a frozen mixture of milk products and flavorings, containing a minimum of 10% milk fat is...

A frozen bananas

C a Popsicle

B ice cream

D snickerdoodles

D

218. *In Monopoly, what's the most expensive property?*

Boardwalk

The longest Monopoly game ever played lasted 1,680 hours (70 days). Our hat's off to you.

B

219. *Where do astronauts park their spaceships?*

at parking meteors

Why don't astronauts get hungry after lift-off? They just had a big launch.

A

220. *Your friend the matador has a dentist appointment and needs you to fill in for him at work. What should you bring?*

a red cape

And a lot of luck. You'll soon find yourself in a stadium, face-to-face with a bull. Who is drawn to red capes.

A

221. *You like to draw houses. Maybe one day you will become…*

an architect

They design and supervise the building of buildings.

C

222. *What's funny about Mickey Mouse's ears?*

They are always facing you…

No matter if Mickey is facing you, or turned to one side, his ears always look the same.

218 In Monopoly, what's the most expensive property?

A Marvin Gardens **C** Park Place

B Marvin Martian **D** Boardwalk

219 Where do astronauts park their spaceships?

A in the ozone **B** at parking meteors **C** on the moon **D** on Planet Parkinglot

Gimme a second, I'm thinking.

220 Your friend the *matador* has a dentist appointment and needs you to fill in for him at work. What should you bring?

A a red cape **C** a ski mask

B a blender **D** a bow and arrow

221 You like to draw houses. Maybe one day you will become...

A an architect **C** a portrait painter

B a custodian **D** a mover and shaker

222 What's funny about Mickey Mouse's ears?

A He can flap them like wings and fly.

C They are always facing you no matter which way he turns.

B He can take them on and off.

D They receive satellite TV.

A

223. *What do flamingos have to do to stay pink?*

eat special foods

Flamingos eat by straining tiny plants and animals out of lake water. Some of these foods turn their feathers pink.

YOU REALLY SHOULD EAT BETTER.

B

224. *Why do many domesticated turkeys drown?*

They look up with their mouths open in rainstorms.

No one ever said that turkeys were smart.

C

225. *Why do woodpeckers pound their beaks against trees?*

They're looking for food or shelter.

Woodpeckers peck wood to find bugs under the bark and to drill holes for their nests.

B

226. *Which of these birds is unable to fly?*

penguin

They're flightless birds — but awesome swimmers! And snappy dressers.

B

227. *This is a true statement about the ostrich.*

They are the fastest two-legged animal.

They can run 45 miles per hour for up to 30 minutes at a time.

223 **What do flamingos have to do to stay pink?**

A eat special foods

C take baths in Kool-Aid

B live in a really sunny place

D flap their wings at least 6 hours a day

224 **Why do many domesticated turkeys drown?**

A They panic while drinking.

C They don't look before they leap.

B They look up with their mouths open in rainstorms.

D high tide

225 **Why do woodpeckers pound their beaks against trees?**

A They're sharpening their beaks.

C They're looking for food or shelter.

B They're warming up for a fight.

D It feels so good when they stop.

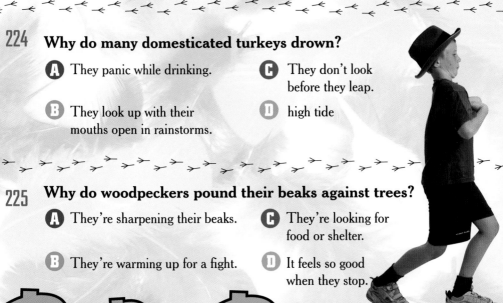

BIRD BRAINS

226 **Which of these birds is unable to fly?**

A chicken

C toucan

B penguin

D wild turkey

227 **This is a true statement about the ostrich.**

A They hide their heads in the sand when scared.

C They have six toes on each foot.

B They are the fastest two-legged animal.

D They make great pets for people who live in apartments.

B

228. I was looking for my tarantula, but it was camouflaged. What's that mean?

blended into the background

A brown spider outside in the dirt and plants is hard to see. It's how many animals hide from predators.

D

229. I put my tarantula on my sister's pillow. When she saw it, she was…

agitated

Upset. Enough said.

C

230. My sister thinks my tarantula is sinister. Meaning what?

up to evil deeds

A long time ago, people who were left-handed were considered sinister. Nowadays, we just see them as goofy.

A

231. Mom says it would be easier to find things like my tarantula if my room were shipshape. Meaning what?

organized

Sailors need to keep things in their proper places to be ready for rough seas.

D

232. My tarantula lost 25% of its legs in a skirmish with the cat. How many legs does it have now?

six

It now has six legs and a fear of cats.

228 I was looking for my tarantula, but it was *camouflaged*. What's that mean?

A sleeping

C changing its skin

B blended into the background

D changing into a butterfly

What's that supposed to mean?

229 I put my tarantula on my sister's pillow. When she saw it, she was...

A elated

B bogus

C serene

D agitated

230 My sister thinks my tarantula is *sinister*. Meaning what?

A carefree

B lost

C up to evil deeds

D smelly

231 Mom says it would be easier to find things like my tarantula if my room were *shipshape*. Meaning what?

A organized

C wet and windy

B out at sea

D clear of furniture

232 My tarantula lost 25% of its legs in a skirmish with the cat. How many legs does it have now?

A one

C four

B eight

D six

CRUNCH!

B

*233. Georges de Mestral invented this while hunting.
He noticed how some prickly plants stuck to his dog's hair.*

Velcro

Way to go, Georges. But the dog should get some credit.

A

*234. Rubber was a sticky, hard-to-use material until Charles Goodyear
vulcanized it. What did he do?*

added chemicals and heat to it

He made rubber harder, more durable and not sticky.
That eventually led to the rubber tire.

D

235. Ezra J. Warner made a lot of hungry explorers happy with this invention.

can opener

Until then many cans were labeled "Cut round the top with
a hammer and chisel" (actual wording taken from a can found
in the Arctic from Robert Peary's expedition).

B

236. Native American George Crum is said to have invented this snack.

potato chips

He was working as a chef. Someone thought
his French fries were too thick. Angry,
he made the thinnest potato slices he
could and fried 'em. People loved 'em.

YOU LIKE US.
YOU REALLY LIKE US!

A

*237. Charles Darrow became the first millionaire
game inventor for this popular board game.*

Monopoly

At first the game was rejected for being too long
and too complicated.

233 Georges de Mestral invented this while hunting. He noticed how some prickly plants stuck to his dog's hair.

A conditioner for dog hair   **C** masking tape

B Velcro   **D** the lawn mower

---

234 Rubber was a sticky, hard-to-use material until Charles Goodyear *vulcanized* it. What did he do?

A added chemicals and heat to it   **C** fed it to Mr. Spock

B threw it into a volcano   **D** wrapped it in plastic

---

235 Ezra J. Warner made a lot of hungry explorers happy with this invention.

A Hot Pockets   **C** soda

B microwave popcorn   **D** can opener

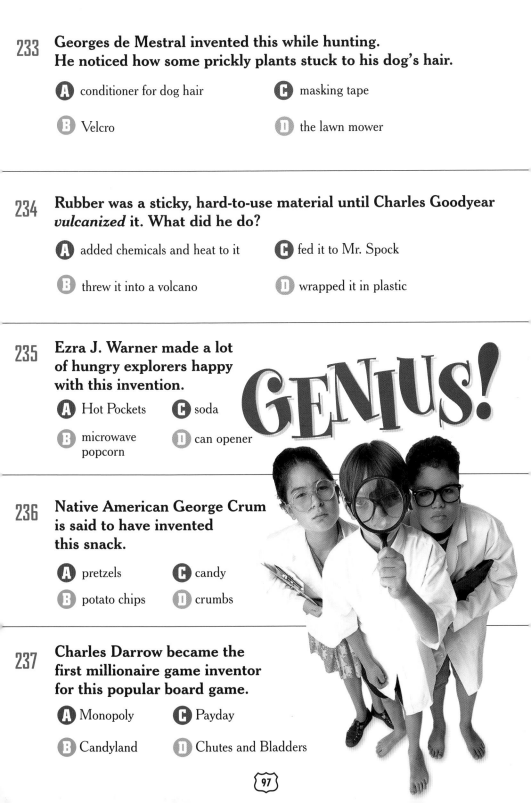

---

236 Native American George Crum is said to have invented this snack.

A pretzels   **C** candy

B potato chips   **D** crumbs

---

237 Charles Darrow became the first millionaire game inventor for this popular board game.

A Monopoly   **C** Payday

B Candyland   **D** Chutes and Bladders

Gary

Sure, he looks great, but he often forgets the names of his clothes.

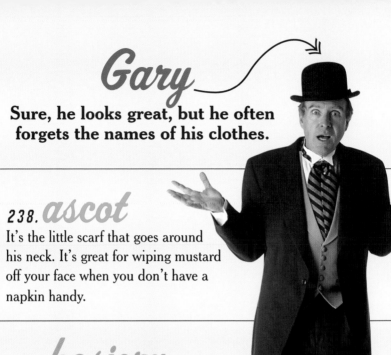

238. *ascot*

It's the little scarf that goes around his neck. It's great for wiping mustard off your face when you don't have a napkin handy.

B

239. *hosiery*

These are his socks or stockings. And Gary shows how the socks really do MAKE the outfit.

D

240. *dress tails*

His jacket has tails. These are useful for wiping the mustard off your ascot should you not have a napkin handy.

C

241. *lapels*

These are the little flaps of fabric on the front of the jacket. Also good for wiping your face, but better used as a place to hide your chewing gum.

A

It's top fashion model *Gary!*

Sure, he looks great, but he often forgets the names of his clothes.

A

B

C

D

238
Where would you find his *ascot?*

239
How about his *hosiery?*

240
Where are his *dress tails?*

241
And where are his *lapels?*

242. *In the middle ages, a new invention arrived from Asia that had an immediate and huge impact on warfare. It was...*

the stirrup

Using stirrups and big saddles, mounted knights holding lances fought like medieval tanks, very difficult to knock down and devastating to men on foot. Without stirrups, knights are like bareback riders — one good blow and off they come.

243. *How did the Barbie doll get her start?*

She was derived from a German doll designed for men.

Barbie is based on a German doll named Lilli, who was designed after a character in a comic strip for men.

244. *Donald Duncan was a businessman vacationing in California in the 1920s when he saw a Filipino bellhop doing something he'd never seen before. Duncan went on to make a fortune with the activity. What was it?*

playing with a yo-yo

Duncan Yo-Yo company sold millions of yo-yos during the Depression. ("If it isn't a Duncan, it isn't a yo-yo.")

245. *In the 1920s, refrigerators contained poisonous gases that occasionally leaked out, killing anyone nearby. A young German scientist read about the problem and patented a better refrigerator. His name was...*

Albert Einstein

He was a teacher of physics at the time at the University of Berlin. It was his last work in the kitchen appliance area.

THANKS AL, FOR A GREAT PLACE TO CHILL.

246. *Who invented television?*

Philo Farnsworth, an Idaho farmboy

Philo T. Farnsworth (1906-1971), who conceived the idea while plowing his family's fields at the age of 14.

A few bright ideas

242 In the middle ages, a new invention arrived from Asia that had an immediate and huge impact on warfare. It was...

A the club

C the bow and arrow

B the boxing glove

D the stirrup

243 How did the Barbie doll get her start?

A She was the brainchild of an American fashion designer.

C She was derived from a German doll designed for men.

B She was based on a movie star of the 50s.

D She is a replica of Queen Victoria.

244 Donald Duncan was a businessman vacationing in California in the 1920s when he saw a Filipino bellhop doing something he'd never seen before. Duncan went on to make a fortune with the activity. What was it?

A grooming dogs

C playing with a yo-yo

B making burritos

D giving sidewalk backrubs

245 In the 1920s, refrigerators contained poisonous gases that occasionally leaked out, killing anyone nearby. A young German scientist read about the problem and patented a better refrigerator. His name was...

A Joseph Frigidaire

C Albert Einstein

B Heinrich Icetray

D General E. Lectric

246 Who invented television?

A Philo Farnsworth, an Idaho farmboy

C Charles Lang, a Chinese-American doctor

B Hendrik Heisenberg, a German scientist

D Sir Phillip van Tele, a British professor

C

247. In what modern professional sport are two- and three-year-olds the very best?

horse racing

Although horses live to twenty or thirty years, their best racing years are when they're two and three. Jockeys, however, are generally adults.

D

248. If your team just won the game by a score of 2-1, what sport were you playing?

hockey

You can't score a single point in football. In volleyball, you have to score 15 to win; in horseshoes, 40.

D

249. Which sport was originally a Native American game?

lacrosse

Lacrosse was played by tribes who considered it excellent practice for war. Games could last for days.

A

250. What sport are you playing if you can pin to win?

wrestling

When you put your opponent's shoulders to the mat, that's a "pin." This guy pinned himself. ˌ– – – – – – –

D

251. The swimming pool game Marco Polo is named after...

an ancient Italian explorer

Marco Polo was a famous Italian explorer who was among the very first to travel from Europe to India. Why his name got attached to a pool game is a little hard to figure.

247 In what modern professional sport are two- and three-year-olds the very best?

A tumbling

C horse racing

B hollering and spit-up

D wrestling

248 If your team just won the game by a score of 2-1, what sport were you playing?

A football

C volleyball

B horseshoes

D hockey

249 Which sport was originally a Native American game?

A basketball

C ice hockey

B golf

D lacrosse

250 What sport are you playing if you can pin to win?

A wrestling

C boxing

B freeze tag

D bowling

251 The swimming pool game Marco Polo is named after...

A Nothing. It's just a made-up name.

C the real game of polo

B a fancy brand of clothes

D an ancient Italian explorer

D

252. Time magazine conducted a poll of historians and writers before the end of the 20th century to name the most influential "Person of the Century." He was…

Albert Einstein

Einstein's name and face are probably the most recognized on Earth. (Challenge: Can you name one other famous scientist?)

A

253. What instrument is generally considered the oldest?

drums

A hollow log that is hit with a stick makes a perfectly fine drum.

A

254. Which is the newest number?

0

The zero we know and love today was invented in India thousands of years after the development of numbers 1 through 9. They needed something to show nothing.

A

255. The world's biggest something weighs 21,140 pounds and is 12 feet in circumference. What is it?

a ball of twine

The world's largest ball of twine is located in Darwin, MN. It was made by one man, Francis A. Johnson, wrapping four hours a day, every day, for 39 years.

C

256. Which of these things is generally considered the oldest?

boomerang

Boomerangs are closely related to "throwing sticks," weapons that were used in many ancient cultures to bring down birds. A boomerang was found in an Egyptian pyramid.

252 *Time* magazine conducted a poll of historians and writers before the end of the 20th century to name the most influential "Person of the Century." He was...

A Pee Wee Herman **C** Adolf Hitler

B Winston Churchill **D** Albert Einstein

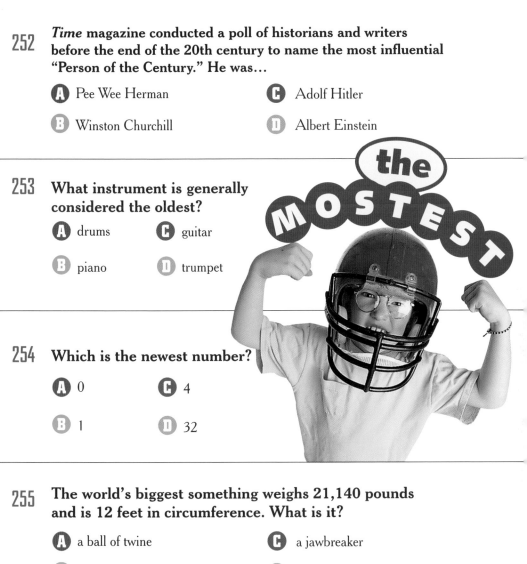

253 What instrument is generally considered the oldest?

A drums **C** guitar

B piano **D** trumpet

254 Which is the newest number?

A 0 **C** 4

B 1 **D** 32

255 The world's biggest something weighs 21,140 pounds and is 12 feet in circumference. What is it?

A a ball of twine **C** a jawbreaker

B a blimp **D** a dust bunny

256 Which of these things is generally considered the oldest?

A bowling ball **C** boomerang

B rubber ball **D** football

C

257. Jupiter, Saturn, Uranus and Neptune are all...

PLANETS MADE OF GAS

They're all gas planets with no solid ground to stand on.

C

258. Which planet is farthest from the sun?

PLUTO

Pluto is usually farthest from the sun, but at times Neptune's orbit takes it farther away from the sun than Pluto.

C

259. At the equator, the Earth is rotating at...

A LITTLE MORE THAN 1,000 MPH

The Earth is about 25,000 miles around. One day — 24 hours — is the time it takes the Earth to make one rotation.

D

260. Why does the moon glow?

IT'S REFLECTING SUNLIGHT.

You won't get a very good tan from the moon, though. Daylight is 500,000 times brighter than full moonlight.

B

261. In 1969 astronaut Alan Shepard did what?

HIT A GOLF BALL TO THE MOON

He cheated a little since he was on the moon when he did it, but still...

257 Jupiter, Saturn, Uranus and Neptune are all...

A planets and car names

C planets made of gas

B inhabited by known life

D college graduates

SPACE

a few questions
that may be over your head

258 Which planet is farthest from the sun?

A Mercury

B Saturn

C Pluto

D Goofy

259 At the equator, the Earth is rotating at...

A 200 miles per hour

B 2,000,000 miles per hour

C a little more than 1,000 miles per hour

D Zero—it doesn't rotate at the equator.

260 Why does the moon glow?

A It's radioactive.

B It's made of glow-in-the-dark cheeses.

C It's hot.

D It's reflecting sunlight.

261 In 1969 astronaut Alan Shepard did what?

A wrote the song "Stardust"

B hit a golf ball to the moon

C landed on Mars

D joined the Moonies and became a follower of the Reverend Sun Myung Moon

262. *Snakes are reptiles. All reptiles are cold-blooded. What does that mean?*

They rely on their environment for body heat.

You are warm-blooded and can generate your own heat. And you can sweat when you get hot to cool off. A snake needs a warm place to stay warm. And a shady place to chill out.

B

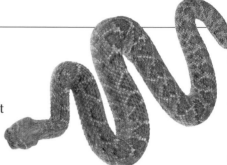

263. *Which of these statements is false?*

Snakes have no skeleton.

They sure DO have a skeleton. It may not have legs and arms, but it does have one beautiful spine and a nifty skull.

A

264. *Which of these things will you never see a snake do?*

blink

Snakes don't have eyelids. They know it's rude to stare, but they can't help it.

D

265. *Most snakes do this only once a week.*

eat

One live rodent goes a long way.

B

266. *Why do snakes shed their skin?*

They get too big for it.

As they grow, they need to get rid of it. Their outer layer of skin is dead, so it won't grow with them.

B

262 Snakes are reptiles. All reptiles are cold-blooded. What does that mean?

A They're mean.

B They rely on their environment for body heat.

C They are cold to the touch.

D They stay cool under pressure.

263 Which of these statements is false?

A Snakes have no skeleton.

B Rattlesnakes can't hear their own rattle.

C Not all snakes have fangs.

D Snakes don't need a lot of space.

264 Which of these things will you never see a snake do?

A eat a live animal

B shed its skin

C eat another snake

D blink

265 Most snakes do this only once a week.

A sleep

B eat

C burp

D floss their fangs

SSSSUPER!

266 Why do snakes shed their skin?

A It goes out of style.

B They get too big for it.

C It gets burned by the sun.

D So their scent doesn't scare away their prey.

C

267. *Lizards have noses, but they smell with their...*

tongues

Snakes do this too. It's fun.

C

268. *Lizards can do this neat trick with their tails.*

grow a new one if it breaks off

If they are attacked, they'll shake loose their tail as a distraction. Then a new one grows back.

B

269. *Dinosaur comes from two Greek words meaning...*

terrible lizard

Those Greeks got it right.

THAT'S RIGHT! I AM BIG TROUBLE.

A

270. *The world's smallest lizard can fit on your fingertip. It is called...*

the dwarf gecko

Awww. It's soooooo cute.
If you like scaly little reptiles.

YO.

B

271. *How does the world's biggest lizard, the Komodo dragon, weighing up to 300 pounds, kill its prey?*

Its saliva contains deadly bacteria.

At 300 pounds it's hard to run after faster animals. It bites its prey once, then just waits for it to drop. Then it digs in.

267 Lizards have noses, but they smell with their...

A eyes

C tongues

B ears

D skin

268 Lizards can do this neat trick with their tails.

A juggle three apples

C grow a new one if it breaks off

B swing from trees

D detect the direction of the wind

Lizards

269 *Dinosaur* comes from two Greek words meaning...

A hungry beast

C huge lizard

B terrible lizard

D run away

270 The world's smallest lizard can fit on your fingertip. It is called...

A the dwarf gecko

C the Gila mini-monster

B the tinysaurous rex

D the mini-gecko

271 How does the world's biggest lizard, the Komodo dragon, weighing up to 300 pounds, kill its prey?

A It just swallows it alive.

C It eats only plants.

B Its saliva contains deadly bacteria.

D It shoots poison out of its eyes.

B

272. Which of these was invented first?

make-up

Everything else came much later. Glasses, around the year 1275, books in 1450, soda pop, around 1767. The ancient Egyptians, in 2000 BC, loved thick eye make-up.

C

273. Throughout history, why has gold always been so valuable?

because it's hard to find

Anything that's extremely rare has greater value. Like old baseball cards.

C

274. How come we don't have any photographs of Napoleon?

Cameras weren't invented yet.

The first photographs ever taken were in France in 1827. Napoleon lived from 1769 to 1821. Just missed it.

A

275. Most scientists think humans came to North America for the first time…

by walking over a land bridge between Alaska and Siberia

Siberians may have been the first humans to see the New World. Between 10,000 and 18,000 years ago, the theory goes, they walked over a strip of land that no longer exists, linking Russia to the United States.

C

276. What do most scientists think killed all the dinosaurs?

a huge meteorite

Most scientists believe a huge meteorite landed off the coast of what's now Mexico and the resulting dust and fires killed off the dinos.

More Historical Stuff

272 **Which of these was invented first?**

A soda pop

C books

B make-up

D eyeglasses

273 **Throughout history, why has gold always been so valuable?**

A because it's a pretty gold color

C because it's so hard to find

B because it's good for making jewelry

D because it's from California

274 **How come we don't have any photographs of Napoleon?**

A He hated cameras.

C Cameras weren't invented yet.

B People lost them over the years.

D He was too short to fit in the frame.

275 **Most scientists think humans came to North America for the first time...**

A by walking over a land bridge between Alaska and Siberia

C with Columbus in 1492

B on a discount airline

D by walking north from South America through Central America

276 **What do most scientists think killed all the dinosaurs?**

A over-hunting by the cavemen

C a huge meteorite

B poor eating habits and lack of exercise

D smoking

B

277. Skunks are nocturnal. What's that mean?

They're awake at night.

They sleep during the day and hunt for food at night.
So if you empty your trash at 2 in the morning, be careful.

B

278. Why do they spray?

They get scared.

It's how they defend themselves,
and it's pretty effective.

THEY'RE NOT THE ONLY ONES!

B

279. Another name for a skunk is…

polecat

What's the best way to call a skunk?
Long distance.

A

280. They warn you before they spray by doing this.

lifting their tails and pounding their front feet

If you ever see a skunk doing this
in your direction, RUN!!!!

B

*281. Dogs are frequent victims of skunk spray. What do many people do
if their dogs get skunked?*

wash the dog in tomato juice

It doesn't really get rid of the skunk smell. But your dog will smell
more like tomato juice than skunk, which is better. But not much.

277 Skunks are *nocturnal*. What's that mean?

A They stink all the time.

C They never sleep.

B They're awake at night.

D They don't eat fish.

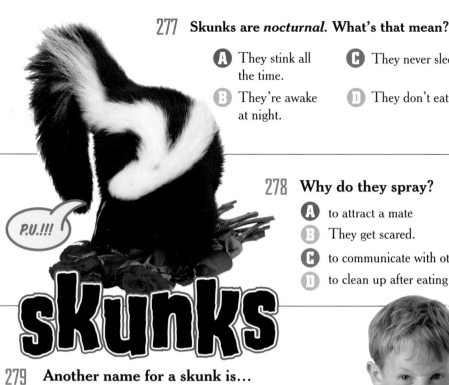

P.U.!!!

skunks

278 Why do they spray?

A to attract a mate

B They get scared.

C to communicate with other skunks

D to clean up after eating

279 Another name for a skunk is...

A stripe-back possum

C smellimal

B polecat

D stinktail

280 They warn you before they spray by doing this.

A lifting their tails and pounding their front feet

C They make hissing and clicking noises.

B spinning wildly in circles

D plugging their noses

281 Dogs are frequent victims of skunk spray. What do many people do if their dogs get skunked?

A get a new dog

C wash the dog in maple syrup

B wash the dog in tomato juice

D shave the dog and put a sweater on it

C

282. *The most popular candy bar today is…*

Snickers

Apparently, according to word on the street...
it really satisfies.

I'LL SAY!

C

283. *If you stir milk long enough, you'll make…*

butter

Stirring milk to make butter, incidentally,
is called "churning."

C

284. *What was the kiwi called before they changed its name in the 1960s?*

Chinese gooseberry

The name change was a smart move.
Popularity soared quite quickly afterwards.

B

285. *In 1954, a milkshake machine salesman named Ray Kroc
went to visit a large customer of his in California. Kroc was so
impressed with the restaurant that he bought it and started a chain,
whose most popular menu item is now called…*

The Big Mac

The Big Mac was born in 1968.

WHAT ABOUT THE BURGER KING?

B

286. *In the 1866, a Mexican businessman helped popularize chewing gum by selling
the raw material to the United States. Before that he…*

led the army that killed Davy Crockett at the Alamo

Antonio Lopez de Santa Anna y Peréz de Lebrón was known as General Santa Anna
at the time. Afterwards, he left the military, tried his hand at politics, and finally ended
up in the chicle export business. Chicle is a special kind of gummy tree sap.

282 The most popular candy bar today is…

(A) the Hershey bar   (C) Snickers

(B) Three Musketeers   (D) Almond Joy

283 If you stir milk long enough, you'll make…

(A) a milk shake   (C) butter

(B) yogurt   (D) Silly Putty

284 What was the kiwi called before they changed its name in the 1960s?

(A) Mongolian thunderfruit   (C) Chinese gooseberry

(B) New Zealand zutnut   (D) Australian apple

285 In 1954, a milkshake machine salesman named Ray Kroc went to visit a large customer of his in California. Kroc was so impressed with the restaurant that he bought it and started a chain, whose most popular menu item is now called…

(A) The Big Kroc   (C) The Big Whopper

(B) The Big Mac   (D) A double latte

286 In the 1860s, a Mexican businessman helped popularize chewing gum by selling the raw material to the United States. Before that he…

(A) invented salsa   (C) discovered the first chihuahua

(B) led the army that killed Davy Crockett at the Alamo   (D) founded the Taco Bell chain

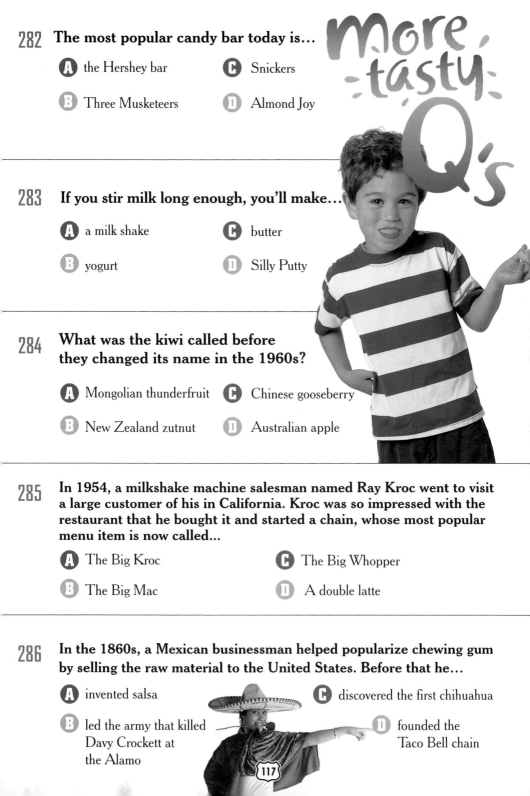

A BIG PILE OF
THANKS
FOR A NICE TRIP

Art Direction:
Jill Turney

Book Design:
Michael Sherman
Maria Seamans

Trivial Types:
Peder Jones
Michael Sherman
Dan Roddick
John Cassidy

Photography:
Peter Fox
Jock McDonald

Traffic Control:
Gary McDonald

Cruise Control:
Carolyn Kemp

Tune Ups:
Patricia Zylius
Stephen Forsling

Tire Kicking:
Karen Phillips

Gas and Snacks:
John Cassidy

CAN'T GET ENOUGH?

Here are some simple ways
to keep the Klutz coming.

1. Get your hands on a copy of **The Klutz Catalog.** To request a free copy of our completely compelling mail order catalog, go to **klutz.com/catalog.**

2. Become a Klutz Insider and get e-mail about new releases, special offers, contests, games, goofiness and who-knows-what-all. If you're a grown-up who wants to receive e-mail from Klutz, head to **klutz.com/certified.**

KLUTZ.com
Come on in!

OPEN 24 HOURS

If any of this sounds good to you, but you don't feel like going on-line right now, just call us at **1-800-737-4123**. We'd love to hear from you.

Still Traveling?

Try these other great books from **KLUTZ**

Books-in-a-Cup™ Lime

Books-in-a-Cup™ Orange

Cat's Cradle® • Doodle Faces

Kids Travel® • *DRAW THUMB ANIMALS*

The Only Activity Book You'll Ever Need

My Anytime Anywhere Autograph Book

My Fabulous Life in Pictures

The Maze Book • **Tricky Pix**